An Alphabet for Dreamers

The MIT Press's publishing mission benefits from the generosity of our donors, including Diana Chapman Walsh.

An Alphabet for Dreamers

HOW TO SEE THE WORLD WITH EYES CLOSED

Sharon Sliwinski   illustrated by Melinda Josie

THE MIT PRESS
CAMBRIDGE, MASSACHUSETTS
LONDON, ENGLAND

The MIT Press
Massachusetts Institute of Technology
77 Massachusetts Avenue, Cambridge, MA 02139
mitpress.mit.edu

The MIT Press would like to thank the anonymous peer reviewers who provided comments on drafts of this book. The generous work of academic experts is essential for establishing the authority and quality of our publications. We acknowledge with gratitude the contributions of these otherwise uncredited readers.

This book was set in Arnhem Pro and PF Din Pro by the MIT Press. Printed and bound in the United States of America.

Library of Congress Cataloging-in-Publication Data

Names: Sliwinski, Sharon, 1975– author. | Josie, Melinda, illustrator.
Title: An alphabet for dreamers : how to see the world with eyes closed /
    Sharon Sliwinski ; illustrated by Melinda Josie.
Description: Cambridge, Massachusetts : The MIT Press, [2025] |
Includes bibliographical references.
Identifiers: LCCN 2024046951 (print) | LCCN 2024046952 (ebook) | ISBN
    9780262049795 (hardcover) | ISBN 9780262383721 (pdf) | ISBN
    9780262383738 (epub)
Subjects: LCSH: Dreams.
Classification: LCC BF1078 .S555 2025 (print) | LCC BF1078 (ebook) |
    DDC 154.6/3—dc23/eng/20250205
LC record available at https://lccn.loc.gov/2024046951
LC ebook record available at https://lccn.loc.gov/2024046952

10   9   8   7   6   5   4   3   2   1

EU Authorised Representative: Easy Access System Europe, Mustamäe tee 50, 10621 Tallinn, Estonia | Email: gpsr.requests@easproject.com

Though we do not wholly believe it yet, the interior life is a real life, and the intangible dreams of people have a tangible effect on the world.

—**James Baldwin,** *Nobody Knows My Name*

CONTENTS

Human beings are dreaming creatures. For much of our history, the images, feelings, and thoughts that come into our minds while we sleep have been understood to be a crucial source of knowledge and an indispensable tool for generating new worlds and new ways of living. The practice of attending to dream life was once considered to be vital to the care of the self, and sharing these visions was thought to be necessary for the social good. Throughout modernity, however, the value of dream life was slowly degraded, especially in the Western world. Our ability to reflect collectively on our past or envision a future has subsequently withered.

This book aims to help restore dreaming to its proper place as one of our most important ways of seeing. Like all alphabet books, the goal is to provide readers with a new grammar—in this case, about the world-making activity called dreaming. Taken together, these chapters offer a series of critical lessons about how to use this imaginative mode of seeing to represent and transform our shared reality. This is a book *of* dreams *for* dreamers.

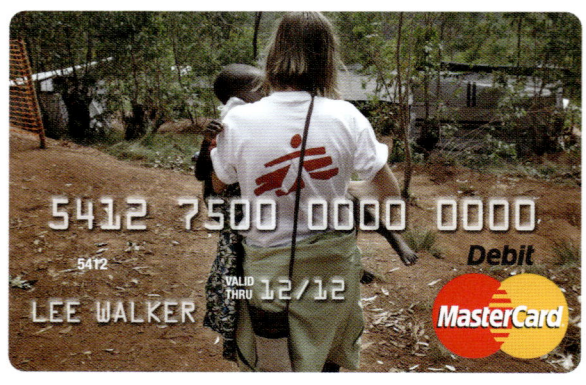

Digital mock-up for a proposed Mastercard debit card.
Original photograph by Martina Bacigalupo/VU, Malaria in
North Burundi, 2009. Courtesy of the photographer.

Martina was in tears on the phone, distraught after having been awoken by a nightmare. She was living in Paris at the time, and I was living in Toronto, so while this was a late-night phone call for me, it was already early morning in France. Martina and I shared an ongoing conversation, so this kind of phone call was not unusual, but her level of distress was worrying. I listened quietly, letting my attention hover evenly as she spoke.

In the nightmare, as Martina described it, she was pedaling a strange sewing-machine-like device. The device was fitted with a long tube that was connected to a child. As she pedaled helplessly in the dream, she saw the child's life slowly draining away. Martina wept as she reported this to me, aghast that she had acted as she did in the dream and that she had envisioned such a horrific scene in the first place.

A little backstory: before she moved to Paris, Martina had spent a decade working as a humanitarian photographer documenting the plight of women and children in conflict zones. As she spoke about her nightmare, I recalled some of the horrific scenes she had witnessed and relayed to me over the years. She mentioned her own daughter, Nina, a joyful child, and began expressing what seemed to be a kind of primal maternal anguish. I tried to offer comfort by reminding her that dreams are carefully designed visions, despite the fact they come unbidden. But my words failed to assuage my friend's feelings of acute remorse.

When I first met Martina, she was nearly ready to give up working as a documentary photographer. As she tells the story, the turning point came when a humanitarian agency asked for permission to reproduce one of her photographs on a credit card. Through a partnership with the credit card company, the humanitarian agency would receive a percentage of the card transaction fees, and the agency felt that this photograph—a picture of a white aid worker holding a black child in her arms—captured the spirit of the agency's supporters. Martina had been exasperated by the racist politics that dominated her field, but this request—which seemed to be an explicit commodification of white saviorism—felt like the point of no return.

It was a shared sense of frustration with the medium that drew us together. Martina and I met at a photography conference that she was attending as a practitioner and I as a scholar. We both were ambivalently invested in the medium. It is hard not to be. The invention of photographic technology revolutionized our ways of seeing. As the British writer John Berger put it, the camera "saves a set of appearances from the otherwise inevitable supersession of further appearances. It holds them unchanging. And before the invention of the camera, nothing could do this, save the mind's eye, the faculty of memory."[1] But as Berger and others have pointed out, this static framing of certain appearances in an instant of time is not how we experience reality. Our living impression of the world is made up thousands of discrete glimpses that build up into a continuous sense of experience.

Despite this difference, the medium of photography has nevertheless come to dominate our way of seeing, eclipsing older ways of engaging and understanding the world. Digital cameras—and especially the ones incorporated into our mobile phones—have become *the* primary medium through which we view each other and the world. And in spite of growing concerns about the synthetic nature of media, we tend to grant these images a certain transparency of meaning. Most of us accept the evidence that these photographs offer, whether a picture is of a friend's birthday party, a colleague's vacation, or a war in a distant country. Despite our differing levels of understanding about the ways these images work to frame reality, most of us share a tacit agreement: these images have come to stand in for reality itself.

But as Martina's dramatic nightmare attests, we also see while we sleep. Indeed, dreams are not just visual experiences but often total environments filled with sound, sensation, and emotions that can leave us breathless. And although we do not always remember them upon waking, most of us dream every night. Given this ubiquity, it is curious that we pay so little attention to these other images, privileging instead the pictures that circulate on our screens.

An Alphabet for Dreamers aims to make a modest intervention into this visual regime. My goal is to return dreaming to its proper place as one of our most important technologies for seeing the world. Like photographs, dreams are transports for critical information, although they convey it in an unusual form. To use the language of the academy, the affordances of this medium are distinct.

Many of us—and especially those of us in the Western world—have lost fluency with this ancient mode of seeing. As a result, we have lost touch with a crucial source of nonrational knowledge. The good news is that we continue to dream, often throughout most of the night (and even while we are awake, although we call that imagination). The gateway to this other way of seeing remains open.

Dreaming Is World-Making

Almost every human culture has its own way of defining the images that come into our mind while we sleep. This book does not attempt to catalog all these methods or to offer a universal theory. As the radical psychiatrist Frantz Fanon suggested, dreams have a "proper time" and a "proper place."[2] These experiences are formed and shaped by each dreamer's unique cultural and historical situation and lived experience. Despite the enduring popularity of the dream book that promises a universal key to interpretation, our nighttime visions are not fashioned from of a static catalog of symbols.

Quite the opposite: in this book, dreaming is treated as one of our most important acts of *world-making*. I use this phrase to emphasize the fact that the world is not a passive thing. We live in a dynamic environment that is constantly changing. And as part of this dynamic environment, we are tasked with making meaning out of our experiences of the world. Awake or asleep, the human psyche never stops working to discern, create, and modify reality. Dreams weave together perception with the manifold of sensation and memory to create a series of images that we see with the mind's eye.

Because they usually occur while we are asleep, dreams seem to be removed from reality, but these visions are one of the crucial means by which we endow our lives with meaning. Dreaming is symbolically akin to inhalation in this respect, an essential process for taking in elements of the external world to create inner reality—part of the way we come alive to life. And in certain contexts, dreaming can also serve as a crucial way to *stay* alive to life. As you will see in some of the chapters that follow, in dark times, these visions can become a potent survival strategy. As one of our last lines of defense, dreams can help hold open a sense of futurity in the face of annihilation.

Given the vast scope of the topic, this book is designed as a primer rather than an encyclopedia—an introduction for those who might wish to know more about how this gossamer way of seeing works. Rather than cleave to any one discipline, I draw from a wide and eclectic range of sources, which makes this book difficult to categorize. I borrow liberally from Sigmund Freud's legacy, although I am more interested in the doctor's method of *attending* to dreams rather than his more famous theory of *interpreting* them. Dreams implicitly teach us to pay attention to what is happening in the theater of the mind. It was this implicit demand to pay attention that inspired Freud's unique method of talk therapy, which he named *psychoanalyse* (psychoanalysis).

Freud's method has been adapted and shaped by subsequent generations of psychosocial practitioners, including Frantz Fanon, whose emphasis on the *socius*—the sociocultural situation of the dreamer—guides my approach here.[3] Fanon spent the entirety of his relatively short career grappling with the colonizing force of his profession, including the ways Western psychologists imposed their singular worldview onto non-Western people under the claim of universality. His attempt to intervene in this violence played out in the way he understood dream life. Fanon's intervention is taken up in more detail in the "H Is for HOMEWORK" chapter, but the psychiatrist suggested that dreams are important because they locate us within the *socius*, revealing the ways we are tethered to the world—for better or worse.

Dreams manifest our unique bond to the social imaginary, but they also provide the means to shift our moorings. Natural law dictates that change and transformation will occur if we pay attention. The presence of an observer changes the dynamic of the situation (whether in psychology or physics). Dreams teach us to adopt this perspective, and in this respect, they are one of our most powerful schools of transformation.

This book is also influenced by some of Freud's fiercest critics, including the French historian Michel Foucault, who despite a lifelong interest in dreams, also wrote about the violently disciplining power of the "psy" professions. But at the end of his life, Foucault returned to dreams and dream interpretation as an important means to investigate what he called the "care of the self." This work also guides my approach here, but many of the most significant lessons in the book are drawn from the radical Black tradition: James Baldwin, Octavia Butler, and Audre Lorde are prominent guides in these pages. And some chapters are in direct dialogue with contemporary Indigenous scholars and practitioners who offer counsel about how to attend to dream life as an explicitly decolonizing practice—Eduardo Duran, Abigail Echo-Hawk, and Leanne Betasamosake Simpson.

As my title suggests, my guiding inspiration is the genre of the alphabet book—that special class of picture books designed to teach people to read (another crucial way of seeing). I have been obsessed with picture books all my life, especially the ones that have very little text. The simple presentation of information in these books can feel like a gift. Creating space for a reader's imagination to wander freely is a powerful lesson in world-making.

Picture books make meaning by combining images and words, often in a way that suggests a sequence of events. Sharing a dream upon waking works in a parallel fashion. The dreamer translates the experience of the dream into language, transposing scenes and feelings into words. Although it can be hard to convey the complexity, the beauty, or the terror that any given dream inspires, this gesture of sharing the experience with someone enables something crucial: a private experience becomes a story.

It is hard to overstate the significance of this relatively simple act. As almost every parent knows, helping a child to relay a nightmare can lessen some of its hallucinatory force. Relief comes to the child because the dream that is captured in words is different from the dream as experienced. Translating the experience of a nightmare into language helps to absorb the shock of the event. This is because the act of narrating a dream (or any experience) subtly reworks our subject-object relations. By narrating a dream, we recreate ourselves as subjects *of* the experience, which allows us to have some purchase over the events. Sharing a dream also turns a solitary experience into something social and situates the dreamer within the larger web of human relationships. This is how I define *world-making*: the act of making words stand in for the world, which is one of the key means by which we transform our subjective experience.[4] Dreaming, and then sharing these visions, is an organic mechanism for changing the moorings of our being within the shared universe of meaning.

The material of dream life is borrowed from existing reality. This imaginary landscape is built from objects that we have perceptually grasped from our environments. For instance, Iris, the eight-year-old at the center of the "K Is for KIDS" chapter, dreams about her iPad, which is the primary tool she used to mediate her experience of the world during the COVID-19 pandemic. Meanwhile, Sergei Pankejeff, the wealthy aristocratic who grew up on an estate in rural Russia that hosted annual wolf hunts at the turn of the twentieth century—who is featured in the "W Is for WHITE WOLVES" chapter—was haunted by a childhood nightmare about, well, wolves. In this respect, dreams can be understood as a kind of cognitive map that locates us in time and space.

But dreams do not simply reproduce the material world. They bring new worlds into being. And what we do with these visions—how we respond to these experiences—is crucial. This process begins when we translate our dreams into words. This relatively simple gesture sets off the spark of transformation, the alchemical process by which we can recreate our sense of self, reconstitute our forms of relationality, and reshape the worlds that we collectively inhabit.

Attending to dream life provides "the leap," as Frantz Fanon would say, that introduces invention into existence.[5]

A Brief Note on Epistemology; or, Why Some People Think Dreams Are Meaningless

Epistemology is an intimidating word that means "the study of knowledge" (the ancient Greek word for *knowledge* is *epistēmē*). This specialized branch of philosophy examines how we know what we know, what counts as knowledge, and what the limitations of any given knowledge system are. Although dreams were understood to be a crucial source of knowledge for most of human history, this ancient episteme was eroded during the scientific revolution.

Beginning in the seventeenth century, Enlightenment philosophers began to see dreams as a problem to be overcome—as a kind of roadblock in the larger effort to develop an objective form of knowledge. For instance, the opening of René Descartes's influential work from 1641, *Meditations on First Philosophy*, begins with the narrator's admission that he finds it difficult to determine the difference between dream and waking reality. This conundrum drives the philosopher's quest to find a more certain ground for knowledge. Often referred to as the "father of epistemology," Descartes privileged certainty above all else, and his resulting philosophical system sought to distinguish "true knowledge" from "false delusions." Cartesianism is often cited as the basis for modern science, with its structure of inquiry that proceeds from doubt to certainty.

There is a backstory to how this new episteme came about. In his early twenties, Descartes began experiencing what we might now call an existential crisis. (At least one biographer calls it a "nervous breakdown.")[6] Feeling adrift and without purpose, Descartes joined the Dutch army as a gentleman volunteer, thinking that the practical experience of war would help expand his horizons. The plan succeeded, although perhaps not as he envisioned. On one particularly cold and miserable night in November 1619, Descartes shut himself up in a room with a large fireplace and was visited by a series of deeply disturbing dreams.

The first was a nightmare in which terrifying phantoms appeared. He tried to drive them away but felt ashamed by a terrible weakness in his right side that disabled him. Lurching along, he was then caught up in a powerful wind and barely managed to stagger into a chapel. When Descartes awoke from this nightmare, he felt a sharp pain in his side. Feeling anxious that he may have erred in the eyes of God, he prayed and reflected on good and evil before falling asleep again, whereupon he immediately had a second dream, which consisted entirely of a great clap of thunder. He opened his eyes to find his room full of sparks, not knowing whether he was asleep or awake. After blinking several times, he was able to get rid of the sparks, and he immediately fell asleep again, relieved.

In the last dream, Descartes dreamt of an encyclopedia laying open on a table. Then he noticed a second book of poetry. As he flipped through the book, one line stood out to him: "Quod vitae sectabor iter?" ("What road in life shall I follow?"). As he was reading, a stranger entered and performed some verses beginning with the words "Est et non" ("It is and is not"). Then just as suddenly, the stranger disappeared.[7]

As biographers have pointed out, Descartes's account closely resembles many well-known classical and biblical dreams in which a young man is faced with a crossroads. Upon waking, the philosopher decided to make it his life's work to finish the poem, so to speak. He quit soldiering and began to evaluate what "is and is not." But rather than give his dreams their due recognition in his new epistemology, Descartes rejected these experiences as akin to the hallucinations of a madman. In his treatise on the nature of scientific knowledge, the philosopher chose to privilege instead the rational, conscious part of his mind—his infamous *cogito*.

Descartes's famous phrase *Cogito, ergo sum* ("I think, therefore I am") is the centerpiece of Cartesian epistemology. Here knowledge is grounded in the indubitability of the ego's existence. The one thing that cannot be doubted, according to the philosopher, is the fact of his existence—and more specifically, the fact of his existence as a "thing that thinks; that is, I am a mind, or intelligence, or intellect, or reason."[8] Descartes's new epistemology, which privileged conscious, rational forms of thought above all else, inaugurated modernity as we know it, setting the foundations for a new definition of scientific knowledge.

I am tempted to correct this received account to say that modernity was in fact born when a fearful and insecure young Frenchman banished the frightening visions that came to him in his dreams. It is not an exaggeration to suggest that this principled rejection of dream life was one of the most disastrous moments in the history of the world. As Cartesian epistemology spread throughout the Western world, reason became the primary seat of human knowledge, and the "thinking" mind became severed from the "unthinking" body. Consciousness slowly became an individualized, closed world.

Something crucial was lost in this shift. Dreams are unsettling experiences by design. These visions circumvent the conscious, "thinking" self, disabling the ego's presumed mastery over knowledge. A kind of otherness—often understood to be a divine force—authors these visions, which can leave us feeling profoundly vulnerable. For thousands of years, these experiences were valued precisely *because* they involved undergoing the trial of being inhabited by this otherness. In the ancient Western world as in many contemporary Indigenous communities, this transcendental nature constitutes these visions as a source of truth. But Descartes rejected this form of nonrational knowledge in his new science and posited instead a new relationship between subjectivity and truth ("I think, therefore I am"). And so dreams became relegated to the realm of irrational experience—mere fantasy and *non*sense.[9]

But the new episteme that Descartes helped to usher in was not free from disquiet. During this same period, European powers invaded the Americas, decimated countless Indigenous populations, radically expanded the trade in enslaved peoples from Africa, and unleased an ongoing operation of resource extraction that has resulted in the destruction of great swathes of the planet—all under the banner of reason. The legacy of this colonial worldview—which has relegated so much human and nonhuman life to the category of nonbeing in order to make it disposable—was integrated in succeeding social orders, bequeathing to us the patriarchal, racialized hierarchies that structure our world today.

How do we escape this I-and-it way of seeing in which everything is presumed to exist for our consumption? Consider the etching made by the Spanish artist Francisco Goya, *El sueño de la razón produce monstruos*. The picture shows a man who appears to have fallen asleep at his desk. Behind him is a cloud of frightening-looking bats and owls. A lynx sits close by, watchfully. Goya spells out his message on the side of the desk: "The Sleep of Reason Produces Monsters."

Goya's etching never fails to bring to my mind a young Descartes so unsettled by his nightmares that he was driven to create an entirely new philosophical method to deprive them of meaning. Goya seemed to recognize that such a magnificent act of hubris could result only in unleashing these nightmares upon the world.

In 2008, the British Nigerian artist Yinka Shonibare offered his own version of Goya's visual statement. Shonibare produced a series of five photographs that are compositionally similar to Goya's etching except that each of Shonibare's models is dressed in a different suit made of wax hollandais (Dutch wax-printed cotton)—one of the artist's signature materials. This mass-produced fabric, which has become synonymous with West African fashion, was originally made by the Dutch to sell in the East Indies. Eventually, production of the fabric was moved to Africa, where it became wildly successful (due, in part, to Ghanaian soldiers who served in the Royal Netherlands East Indies Army and returned home with bolts of the fabric). In Shonibare's hands, the material makes visible the ways that the complex legacies of colonialism, with all its displacements and disruptions, have come to structure our everyday lives.

Shonibare also modified Goya's title. In his series of photographs, the writing on the side of the desk is in French, and he adds a location. In one photograph from the sequence, the text reads, "Les songes de la raison produisent-ils des monstres en Afrique?" ("Do the Dreams of Reason Produce Monsters in Africa?"). Other photographs in the series picture different men and reference different continents. Shonibare's question, in dialogue with Goya's statement, draws attention to the uneven

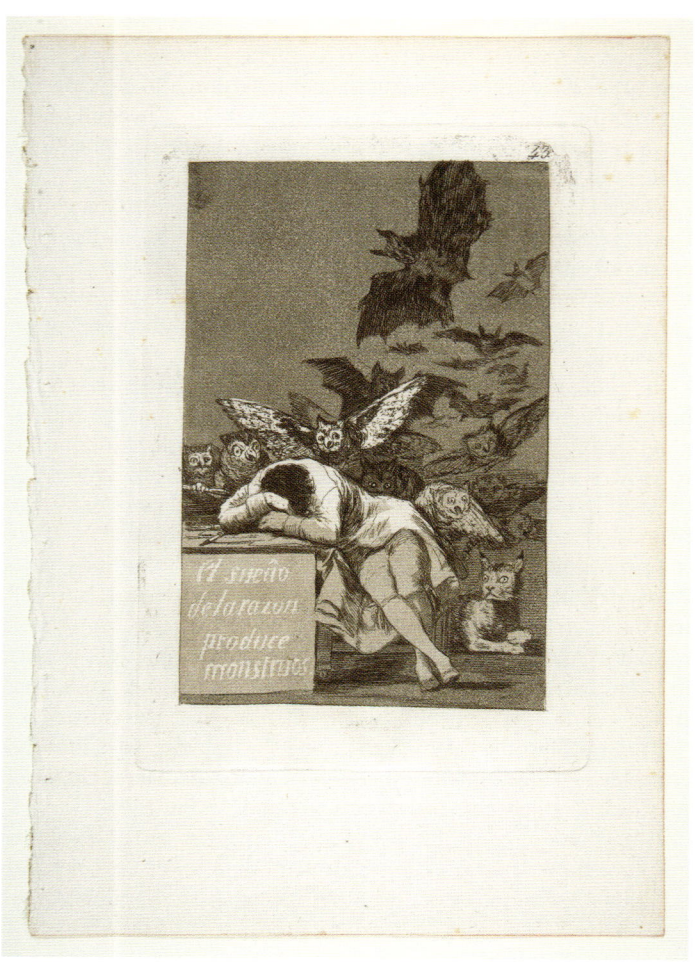

Francisco José de Goya y Lucientes, *El sueño de la razón produce monstruos*, 1799, etching and aquatint. Courtesy of the Metropolitan Museum of Art, gift of M. Knoedler & Co., 1918.

geopolitics of this nightmare. Taken together, these works offer a compact lesson in the ways that reason has *failed* to see.

Artists like Goya and Shonibare teach us to picture what Anibal Quijano has called the "coloniality of power."[10] These works reveal how our habitual ways of seeing, knowing, and being have come to be structured and how one singular worldview (European, white, male) was imposed onto others under the guise of a universal rationality. This recognition makes space for the restitution and revitalization of other histories, practices, languages, and subjectivities—other ways of seeing and knowing that have never ceased challenging this form of violence.

Dreams are central to the history of epistemology because they are a nightly reminder that we are inhabited by an otherness at our core. To adapt one of Freud's phrases, dreams unsettle the idea that the ego can ever be "master in its own house."[11] (The problematic overtones of Freud's terms are intended.) These visions provide proof of the cogito's profound frailty and also expose the dreamer to a form of knowledge that cannot be reached through reasoning or rational examination. Attending to these experiences offers another way to relate to oneself and another way of seeing the world.

The fact that dreams force us to tarry with this fundamental otherness is, in part, why this landscape remains resistant to colonial forms of domination. I am tempted to describe the domain of dream life as *ungovernable*. If we cannot claim sovereignty over our own psyche, how can we claim sovereignty over another? This may be why so many oppressed peoples have attuned themselves to their dream life in their struggles against oppression.

In the case of the Anishinaabeg, the Indigenous people of the Great Lakes region of Canada—the land on which I was born and continue to reside as a settler guest—dreaming never stopped being a crucial medium for the transmission of transcendental forms of knowledge. In Anishinaabeg culture, dreams are cherished as a central mode of learning and reflection about how to be, what to do, and how to contribute to your community.

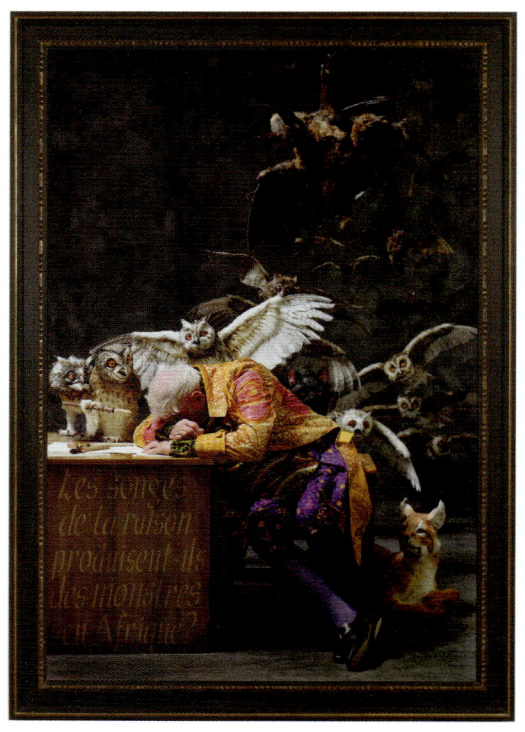

Yinka Shonibare, *The Sleep of Reason Produce Monsters (Africa)*, 2008, chromogenic print mounted on aluminum. Image courtesy James Cohan Gallery.

INTRODUCTION

As Leanne Betasamosake Simpson writes, these visions are important not only because they provide Anishinaabeg dreamers with knowledge of the spiritual world but also because they bring new worlds into being: "dreams provide glimpses of decolonized spaces and transformed realities that we have collectively yet to imagine."[12]

An Alphabet of Dreams for Dreamers

A few words about how this book came to be. In 2020, I was scheduled for a sabbatical. My study plan involved tracing a more precise history of what happened to dream knowledge throughout the European Enlightenment. My goal was to find something that would enable a disruption of the dominant paradigm. If Descartes's rejection of the knowledge bequeathed by his dreams marked the birth of scientific rationality, perhaps some "anomaly," in Thomas Kuhn's sense, might allow for a rethinking of this paradigm. My hope was to find a path back to dream knowledge and the decolonial possibilities it might hold—to find a way to repair if not escape the Cartesian split, the mechanistic dualism that divorced matter from spirit and body from soul.

And then it happened. By spring of 2020, when stay-at-home directives were in widespread effect, social media began to be filled with new hashtags: #lockdowndreams, #coviddreaming, #virusdreams. Even mainstream media outlets began reporting on the global increase in vivid dreams, which seemed to be prompted by anxiety about the COVID-19 pandemic. There had been studies documenting the way extreme events can produce a widespread change in the patterns of dream life, but as Tore Nielsen noted at the time, a "dream surge" of this magnitude had never been seen before.[13] The coronavirus changed how much we were dreaming, but it also changed the nature of dreaming itself. For one of the first times in living memory, the whole world seemed to be dreaming about the same thing—albeit unevenly. The pandemic became a worldwide dreaming event.

This unprecedented situation provided important evidence about the porous relationship between inner life and external reality. This was clear to the many people who noticed a change in their dream life during this time. Their nightly visions seemed to be in direct dialogue with whatever was happening during the grind of the day. This is reflected in one of the metaphors frequently used to describe dream life: *seismographic*. The metaphor recalls the ancient diagnostic function of dreams (discussed in more detail in the "Q Is for QUACKERY" chapter), which can register what is happening at a subterranean or unconscious level.[14] During the pandemic, dream life became one of our principal technologies for processing the meaning of this global event as it unfolded and one of our primary venues for managing the uncertainty of the time. To my eyes, the global surge of interest in dream life seemed to represent a collective moment of recognition, however brief and nascent, of the importance of this other way of seeing.

During this period, I had the good fortune of being invited into a partnership with a curator who was collecting COVID ephemera for the Museum of London in the UK. I gathered a small team of scholars and health professionals to collect oral testimony from Londoners about how the pandemic was affecting their dream life. These conversations with strangers proved to be transformative. After the first round of interviews, which took place by video call, we realized that dream life was serving as a crucial venue for helping people make sense of what was happening. Dreams were providing a kind of attentional prosthesis—a way to look *at* the strangeness of reality (rather than our usual mode of looking *through* it). And without really realizing it at the time, I found that listening to strangers speak about their dream life was also teaching me to see the world in a new way.

One of the aims of this book is to pass on some of these unexpected lessons. In these pages, you will meet some of the Londoners that we interviewed during that time. Their full testimonies are available in the Museum of London's permanent collection, but the handful included here are exemplary for the way these visions shift habitual forms of attention, showing how dreams provide another way to understand what is happening in the world.

The book features these contemporary dreamers alongside other exemplars from the historical record. My goal is to highlight the various ways that people have put their dreams to work and to show how these experiences bolster our fundamental human capacity to imagine new worlds and new ways of being. You may recognize some of these dreamers (and perhaps even some of these dreams), but I suspect most will be unknown to you. In making choices about whom to include in the book, I have kept in mind the urgent need to decenter the subject that the Caribbean writer, Sylvia Wynter, once described as always already overrepresented—"Man."[15]

By privileging different voices, I highlight the critical forms of knowledge that have long resisted the coloniality of power and see what new possibilities might emerge if we collectively attuned ourselves to underrepresented voices. This involves revising "the descriptive statement of the human," in Wynter's terms. The choice to privilege different discursive and performative acts may enable the emergence of new social, symbolic, and political orders. Language is not just descriptive. Certain forms of speech work performatively. They have the power to restructure relationships and ways of being and actively change the constitution of the world.

These chapters introduce vocabulary that I hope will serve the collective effort to reenvision a common world—but mostly they are about the dreamers. The book relies heavily on storytelling because dreams emerge from a living, breathing context, from the vast a web of human experiences that make up a life. In reconstructing these narratives, I have strived to set the stage in a way that gives each dream room to breathe. Rather than try to interpret these visions, I invite you, the reader, to lend your ear and imagination, to *attend* to the dreams so that together we might breathe life back into these narratives.

In my mind, there is something compellingly conspiratorial about this form of collective attunement. The roots of the English word *conspiracy* come from the Latin word *conspirare*, meaning "those who breathe together."[16] Listening to someone report a dream is an act of attuning oneself to another's lifeworld—akin to breathing together. Considering the desperate cries that have been echoing from the streets in recent years—especially the heartrending plea, "I can't breathe"—such an attunement might be understood as a gesture of solidarity, a way to affirm our attachment and connection to others.

A great deal of violence stems from how people have been conditioned to see one another. Dreams offer another way seeing that happens with our eyes closed. These strange, elemental visions have a great deal to teach us about the power of imagination and our capacity to reenvision a just world. As the dreamers gathered here persuasively show, attending to this landscape is one of the most important means by which we can transform ourselves *and* the shared world that lies between us. This radical way of seeing—and the knowledge it can yield—is sorely needed for our collective survival.

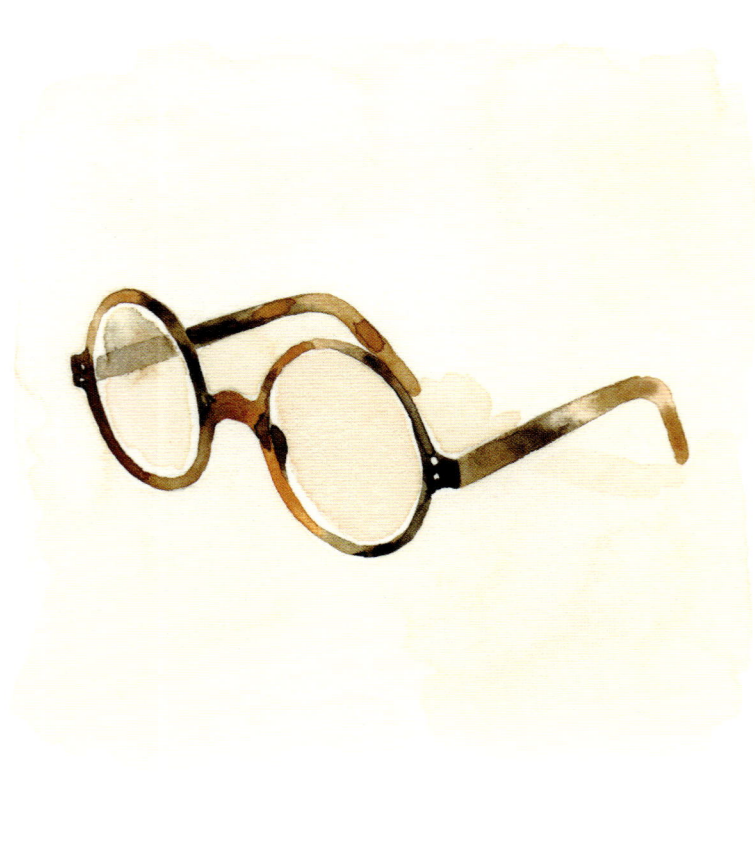

A IS FOR ATTENTION

"What does it mean?" Whenever I find myself talking with someone about dream life, this question invariably arises. I hear it regularly in conversations with strangers, especially on planes and trains. Once people learn about my interest, they often share one of their dreams with me. The generosity of the gesture always astonishes me. Sometimes these strangers tell me about a recurring dream they have had for many years. Sometimes they tell me about a recent nightmare that has disturbed them. And then comes the heartfelt question: "What do you think it means?"

The other figure who regularly turns up in these conversations is the doubter. This skeptic insists that dreams don't mean anything and are simply the brain's way of ridding itself of unwanted thoughts—"mentally flushing the toilet," as someone once vividly put it to me. A striking example of this kind of response came after I gave a presentation at a small liberal arts college in the United States. My discussion focused on one of the nightmares Nelson Mandela reports in his autobiography, *Long Walk to Freedom*. At the end of the allotted time, my host—the chair of the political science department—stood up and joked: "Aren't nightmares just a result of having eaten a bit of bad meat? Ha ha. Well, in any case, I would like to thank you for coming, Professor Sliwinski. Everyone, please join us for a reception next door."

I hear this kind of dismissal a lot. We might classify the department chair's comment as a "negation"—a way to verbally distance himself from the content of my presentation. People regularly deploy this defense mechanism to dismiss something that they perceive to be threatening. The idea that dreams might offer important knowledge is felt to be threatening by some people (perhaps especially by scholars who have been trained to privilege rational forms of thought).

Skepticism about dreams has a long history that can be traced back to antiquity. The idea that dreams are simply a means to rid the mind of unwanted thoughts was proposed in the scientific literature as recently as 1983, when Francis Crick and Graeme Mitchinson published an article in the journal *Nature* suggesting that dream sleep was an occasion for "unlearning."[1] Crick and Mitchinson's view was that the purpose of dreaming is to rid the brain of seemingly superfluous information.

Western science has come full circle on this thesis. Over the last twenty years, psychologists and neuroscientists have found compelling evidence to show that dreaming represents a crucial biological and emotional means for processing experience and that it helps with learning, cognition, emotional regulation, and the consolidation of memories.[2] Some scientists argue that dreams also furnish us with skills that enable us to be more responsive to future events, giving scientific weight to the ancient idea that dreams offer a glimpse of events that are yet to pass. The Brazilian neuroscientist Sidarta Ribeiro, for instance, describes dreams as "oracles of the night," arguing that these visions allow us to predict future events through the reorganization of previous experiences—the opposite of Crick and Mitchinson's claim.[3] In this respect, the contemporary scientific view has come back to Sigmund Freud's initial idea that dreaming is simply "a particular *form* of thinking" that happens while we are asleep.[4]

In contrast to the skeptic's disavowal of dreams, the question "What does it mean?" is important because of the epistemological position of the questioner. In other words, dreams have a way of putting the dreamer in a questioning frame of mind. They sideline our ever-defensive ego and kindle a sense of curiosity, opening us up to uncertainty. In this respect, dreams are experiences that call for a different form of attention. They train us to see differently.

It is hard to overstate how important this frame of mind is and how rare it is for us to lower our ego defenses. If we allow this way of seeing to form the basis of how we act, then the importance of this epistemological position becomes clear.

Each time someone poses this heartfelt question to me, my response is the same. I express my own wonderment about the dream they have reported and then return the query to the dreamer: "What do *you* think it means?" This is meant as a gesture of solidarity—to reinforce these dreamers' sense of curiosity and to encourage them to attend more closely to the details of the dream. A rich and surprising conversation almost always follows.

Part of what drives the question "What does it mean?" is the common idea that dreams require an act of interpretation to reveal their meaning. Indeed, the art of interpreting dreams is as old as humanity itself. The strangers who disclose their visions to me are, in a way, treating me like an expert who might be able to help decipher the mystery. But I also hear something else behind this question. To my ear, the query offers evidence of the way dreams *themselves* issue a powerful directive to pay attention. These visions are usually accompanied with an implicit instruction to observe what is happening in the theater of the mind. When we awake from a dream, we tend to intuitively feel that we have been shown something important—even if the meaning of the vision is far from transparent.

One of Freud's most important contributions was to situate this implicit directive at the center of his therapeutic model. While he often is remembered for his method of interpreting dreams, as the title of his most famous book emphasizes, to my mind, the more significant contribution is his unique theory of *attending* to interior life, his way of *listening* to the images and thoughts that pass through the mind.

Freud's famous psychoanalytical method of treatment was radical for its time and remains radical today. Rather than issue prescriptions, the physician listened attentively to his patients, most of whom were women. Freud understood the power of attention (which in our digital era has become a matter of considerable economic value). The only instruction the doctor gave his patients was to speak about everything that came to mind, regardless of whether it made any sense. Especially welcome were dreams and all the associated thoughts and feelings that these visions elicited. Freud named this process "free association," and it became the fundamental rule of his new therapeutic method.

This gesture of turning attention inward and toward the images and thoughts that enter the mind while asleep is something that is shared among many cultures throughout human history. But in the highly ordered, patriarchal world of nineteenth-century Vienna, Freud's approach was considered revolutionary and itself became subject to repression. The practice of encouraging women to speak openly about what was on their mind was considered to be a threat to the prevailing order. Almost from the outset, psychoanalysis was denigrated as a Jewish science and attacked from all quarters, including by the Nazis, from whom Freud's family was eventually forced to flee.

For this reason, among others, Freud refrained from explaining his therapeutic innovation for more than a decade, much to the frustration of fellow practitioners. In a technical paper published in 1912, he finally outlined his clinical method in detail. In this paper, called "Recommendations to Physicians Practicing Psycho-analysis," Freud introduces a German term to describe his special mode of listening: *gleichschwebende Aufmerksamkeit*. The term is not easy to translate. Freud's English translators opted for "freely floating attention." But the term also has musical connotations as well as a sense of a revolving, circling motion, suggesting an "evenly hovering" or "evenly suspended" form of attention.[5]

By using this term, Freud was trying to distinguish a kind of attention that refrains from focusing on specific details. The danger with concentrated or poised forms of attention is that we often fail to notice things that we are not already expecting to see. Focusing too closely on one thing can make us blind to other things. (Think of people who walk down the street absorbed in their phones.) Freud offers a warning to fellow practitioners about this kind of focused attention: if the therapist listens in a poised way that follows personal expectations, "he is in danger of never finding anything but what he already knows."[6]

Freud's model of free-floating attention, in contrast, describes a state of open receptivity, an evenly distributed form of attention that gives equal notice to all perceptions and that actively withholds influences that would interfere with this receptivity. Freud's advice is to "simply listen" without trying to "hold" anything in mind.[7] Contemporary therapeutic clinicians have extended this model to describe a kind of listening in which listeners actively divest themselves of memory, desire, and understanding.[8]

The radical state of receptivity that Freud cultivated in his therapeutic practice is precisely the kind of attention that dreams intuitively enkindle—an openness to meaning, a tolerance and responsiveness to the unknown: "What does it mean?"

This state of receptivity is also foundational for any genuinely transformational politics. In fact, withholding this form of attention is often understood to constitute a form of epistemological violence. In his book *Hungry Listening: Resonant Theory for Indigenous Sound Studies*, the Stó:lō scholar Dylan Robinson offers a striking account of how listening can falter and fail along these lines. In 1997, the Gitksan and Wet'suwet'en peoples of the Pacific Northwest sued the government of Canada for recognition of their title to land that they have lived on for thousands of years. During the trial in the Supreme Court of Canada, one of the lawyers representing the Indigenous communities invited the Gitksan chief, Mary Johnson, to sing for the court—a recognized mode of submitting evidence under Gitksan law. The presiding judge in the trial, Allan McEachern, objected, saying he did not want a "performance" in his court of law: "'I can't hear your Indian song, Mrs. Johnson. I've got a tin ear.'"[9]

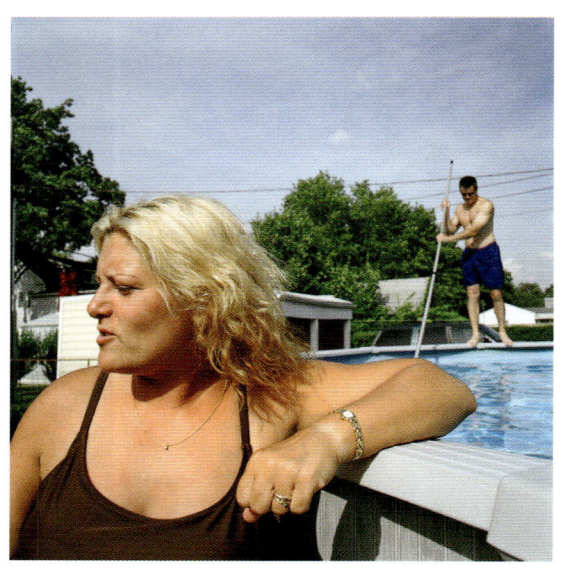

Myra Greene, *A.G., Rochester, New York (2007)*, 2007–2012,
inkjet print. Courtesy of the artist.

A IS FOR ATTENTION

This is a spectacular example of the failure to attune to the other—a refusal to hear something that one doesn't "already know." But this kind of perceptual breakdown occurs in less dramatic, more everyday ways too. In my introductory classes on visual culture, I often show some of Myra Greene's photographic work. I don't preface the exercise with an explanation or with information about the photographer. I show the images and ask students to tell me what they see.

Often this request is met with silence. Students aren't used to being asked to describe photographs because these kinds of images are usually assumed to be self-evident. But eventually, after some coaxing, at least one student will begin describing what they see: "I see a woman with blonde hair leaning against a pool. In the background, a man is standing on the edge of a pool with a long pole." Other students usually start murmuring at this point and join the conversation, deciphering meaning from the details—the woman's jewelry indicating her marital status, the garage buildings that suggest a suburban setting, the aboveground pool that suggests a working-class household, and so on.

Depending how the conversation goes, I sometimes show more images from Myra Greene's series, and we repeat the exercise. Sometimes I directly challenge the students with a question borrowed from the sociologist Tressie McMillan Cottom: "What kind of person has blonde hair?" My goal is to open a conversation about unspoken racial codes. As McMillan Cottom has argued, "we use 'blonde' to signal that someone is white without using a racialized term like 'white,'" although simply voicing this unmarked equation can draw resistance. (McMillan Cotton has been publicly accused of being a racist and banned from social media platforms for daring to mention the whiteness of white people.)[10] Blonde is a discursive strategy to talk about race without talking about race.

One of the aims of Greene's photographic project, which is called "My White Friends," is to draw attention to race as a force that structures *how* we see and *what* we see. While Western viewers have become accustomed to noticing racial differences, as Richard Dyer pointed out thirty years ago, noticing race tends to mean noticing the race of people who are not white: "Other people are raced," Dyer facetiously announced: "we are just people."[11] In other words, whiteness has a way of making itself invisible. A power structure is built into this way of seeing. The invisibility of whiteness allows this racial category to function as the norm. So long as white people are "just people," they retain the authority to speak—and act—on behalf of a universal humanity.

My students and I go on to discuss the politics of representation and display and the ways these matters are governed by power. My goal is to help them learn to train their attention inward as much as outward and to become aware of what Nicholas Mirzoeff has called "white sight"—the cultural unconscious of whiteness that projects and sustains a particular version of reality.[12] This is both an exercise in critical reflexivity and a task that aims to nurture a different, "evenly suspended" kind of attention—a means to instill a kind of openness in their practices of looking and listening. The goal is to learn to actively withhold ideas and desires that interfere with perception—to notice the things that block what is given to be seen and heard.

So many of our received ways of seeing and listening have become burdened by what we believe we "already know." Dreams, in contrast, nurture a radical state of receptivity. These experiences solicit a form of attention that transcends the familiar circuits of expectation, which divests from the well-worn equation that links "seeing" to "knowing."

At least this is what I hear in that repeated, achingly sincere question: "What do you think it means?" Dreams entreat us to lower our defenses and orient us to the world anew. They are a clarion call to adopt a different way of seeing.

B IS FOR BOA CONSTRICTOR

The central idea animating this book—that dreams offer a radical way of seeing—should properly be credited to the picture books of my childhood. I could name many titles that taught me this lesson, but perhaps the best-known example is *Le Petit Prince* (1943), known in the English-speaking world as *The Little Prince*. (The book is a perennial best-seller, but if you haven't yet read it, find a copy immediately.)

The story opens with an unnamed narrator describing a momentous encounter that he had when he was six years old with the picture of a boa constrictor swallowing an animal, which he saw in a book called *True Stories from Nature*. The narrator learns from the book that these snakes swallow their prey whole and then sleep for months to digest their meal. This remarkable fact inspired the six-year-old to produce his first drawing, which he proudly titled *My Drawing Number One*.

The six-year-old's sense of elation about his creation was crushed when the grownups looked at his drawing and saw only a hat. It was then, the narrator tells us, that he realized that grownups always need to have things explained. So he produced a second drawing, which he titled *My Drawing Number Two*.

Once again, however, the grownups' imagination failed. When he revealed his second drawing, the boy was advised to "devote himself to geography, history, arithmetic, and grammar." And so, the narrator tells us, he gave up drawing and studied to become a pilot. But he never forgot this other way of seeing and occasionally tried showing his *Drawing Number One* to new people he met. The experiment always had the same result. The adults always said, "That is a hat."

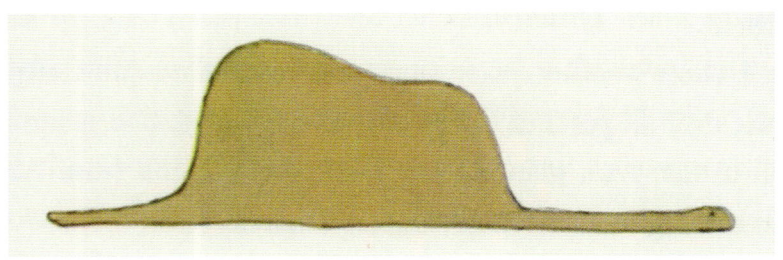

Antoine de Saint Exupéry, *Mon dessin numéro un*, drawing,
Le Petit Prince, 1943. Reprinted by kind courtesy of the
Saint Exupéry/d'Agay estate.

B IS FOR BOA CONSTRICTOR

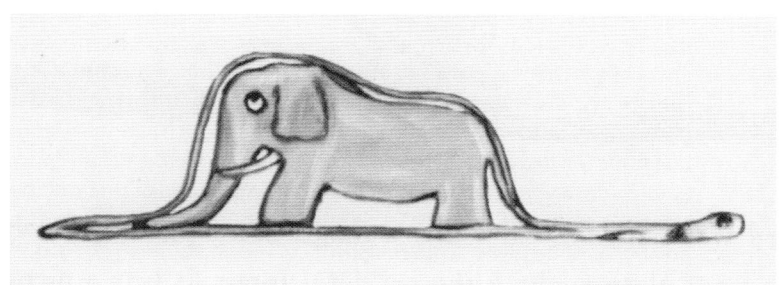

Antoine de Saint Exupéry, *Mon dessin numéro deux*, drawing,
Le Petit Prince, 1943. Reprinted by kind courtesy of the
Saint Exupéry/d'Agay estate.

Many years later, when the pilot's plane broke down and he made an emergency landing in a desert, he finally encountered someone else who could see that dimension of the visible world that is not given to sight.

So begins the story of *The Little Prince*.

This opening scene offers a compact lesson about the power of the imagination and the way our most powerful way of seeing involves the mind's eye. Philosophers have various ways of describing the activities of the imagination, but this faculty always involves the power to create a mental image of something that is not directly present and the ability to transform existing images or ideas into something new. In the introduction to her novel *Frankenstein; or, The Modern Prometheus* (1818), Mary Shelley describes the power of imagination as consisting of "the capacity of seizing on the capabilities of a subject, and in the power of moulding and fashioning ideas suggested to it."[1] (The dream that gave rise to this terrifying novel is discussed in the "M Is for MONSTER" chapter.)

There is something miraculous and yet quotidian about the imagination. Without realizing it, we exercise this mode of seeing all the time, whenever we remember, problem solve, play, invent, daydream, pretend, fantasize, or envisage better times to come. The effortless exercise of our imagination allows us to create and move through our everyday existence. As the philosopher Friedrich Schelling put it, imagination is the "unconscious poetry of being."[2]

This book is concerned with one particular species of imaginative activity—dreaming. Typically, this form of imagining happens while we are asleep, although as the psychoanalyst Wilfred Bion once pointed out, dreaming also occurs while we are awake, albeit unconsciously (a dimension that grownups have difficulty acknowledging).

As I allude to in the "A Is for ATTENTION" chapter, several things make dreams uniquely important, not least of which is that they circumvent our conscious will. Dreams do not rely on rational thinking processes. The images, feelings, and sensations that occur in dreams arrive in consciousness unbidden, and as a result, these experiences implicitly demand a kind of attentiveness. They encourage us to pay attention to them, which positions the self in a different relationship to knowledge. Dreams put the dreamer in a *receptive* (rather than *possessive*) orientation to the world.

The other singularly important aspect of dreaming is the way these visions *transfigure* reality, giving our experiences a new form. This transformational capacity is one of the most important features of dream life. Dreams are a school of metamorphosis. If we are attentive to these visions, they can teach us a great deal about that governing principle of our universe—*change*.

In his clinical work, Sigmund Freud noticed that the content of our dreams often contains "day residues." Our visions are built from perceptions and elements of our daily life. The doctor also recognized that these elements undergo a transformative process to become the manifest content that we experience as a dream. Freud named this process "the dreamwork" (*Traumarbeit* in German), and he frequently argued that this process of transformation was "the essence" of dreaming.

Under the heading of dreamwork, Freud identified four distinct operations of transformation—condensation, displacement, symbolization, and secondary revision. These four operations have their own complex definitions, but what is really at stake here is a theory of change. Dreams transform the raw materials—the day residues—from which they are made, and in so doing, these visions create new meaning out of our experiences. This book is full of examples of the transformative power of dreamwork, and while the clinical theory is fascinating, the best teacher for how this works is picture books.

Do you remember the opening scene of Lewis Carroll's 1871 classic *Through the Looking-Glass*—the sequel to his *Alice's Adventures in Wonderland* (1865)? It begins with a white kitten contentedly having its face washed by its mother while a black

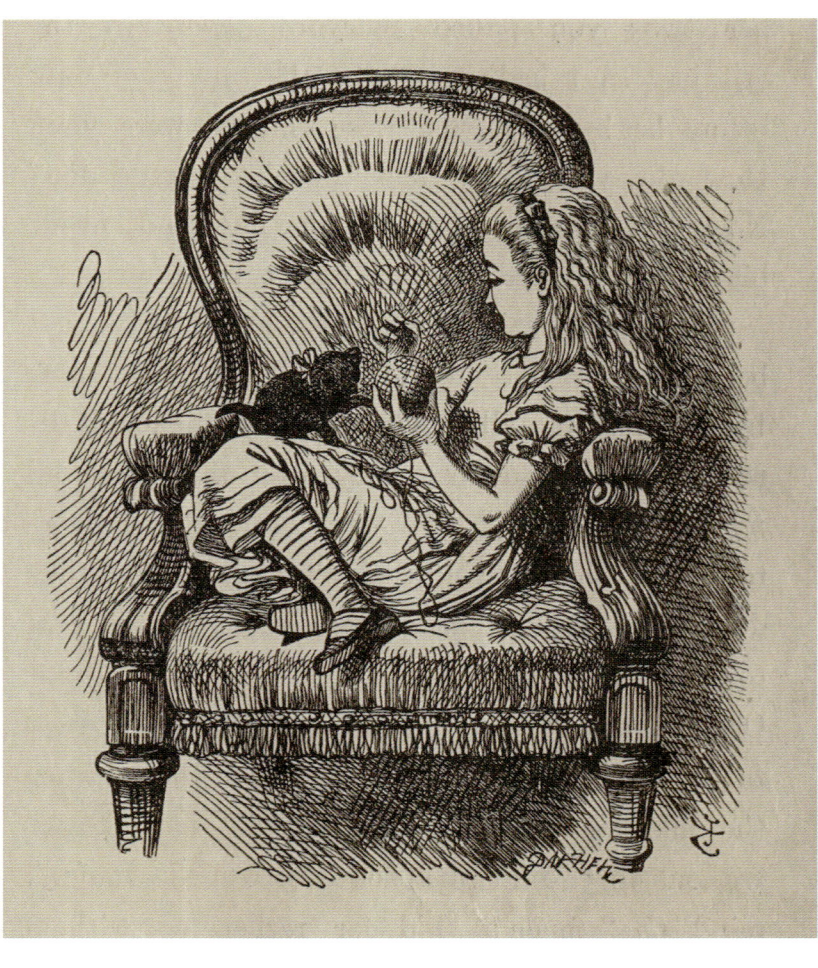

John Tenniel, *Alice and the Black Kitten*, wood engraving,
Lewis Carroll, *Through the Looking-Glass*, 1871.
Courtesy of the Library of Congress.

kitten gets into mischief. After the black kitten unravels of a ball of yarn, Alice finally catches and chastises the kitten to try to make it understand that this grand game of romps is disgraceful: "You wicked wicked little thing!" But in the middle of this exchange, Alice becomes distracted by something she sees in the large mirror that sits on the mantel. She climbs up to make a closer inspection and—poof! She passes right through into Wonderland.

The book ends where it began. The last scene in Wonderland involves a chaotic dinner party with plates that fly, forks that walk, and guests who end up in the soup—all seemingly at the command of the troublesome Red Queen. Just as things are about to get completely out of hand, Alice turns to the Red Queen and picks her up as if to shake sense into her. Once Alice gets her hands on her, however, the Queen begins to grow "shorter—and fatter—and softer—and rounder—and—." The chapter ends abruptly midsentence. The reader turns the page to find one of John Tenniel's beautiful illustrations, which needs no explanation. The text continues: "—and it really *was* a kitten, after all."

Having woken up from a wondrous dream, Alice finds herself back in the drawing room, pondering who created the remarkable world she has just returned from: "Who do you think dreamed it all?" she asks the naughty black kitten, who ignores the query and returns to its mischief with the yarn. Alice protests: "This is a serious question . . . You see, Kitty, it *must* have been either me or the Red King. He was part of my dream, of course—but then I was part of his dream, too!" The book ends before the question is resolved. In fact, the story concludes with an unexpectedly direct appeal to the reader: "Which do *you* think it was?"

At the risk of sounding like a grownup who needs explanations for things that are perfectly self-evident, Lewis Carroll's famous story offers a clear illustration of Freud's concept of the dreamwork. Carroll's books are sometimes described as nonsense literature in much the same way that dreams are

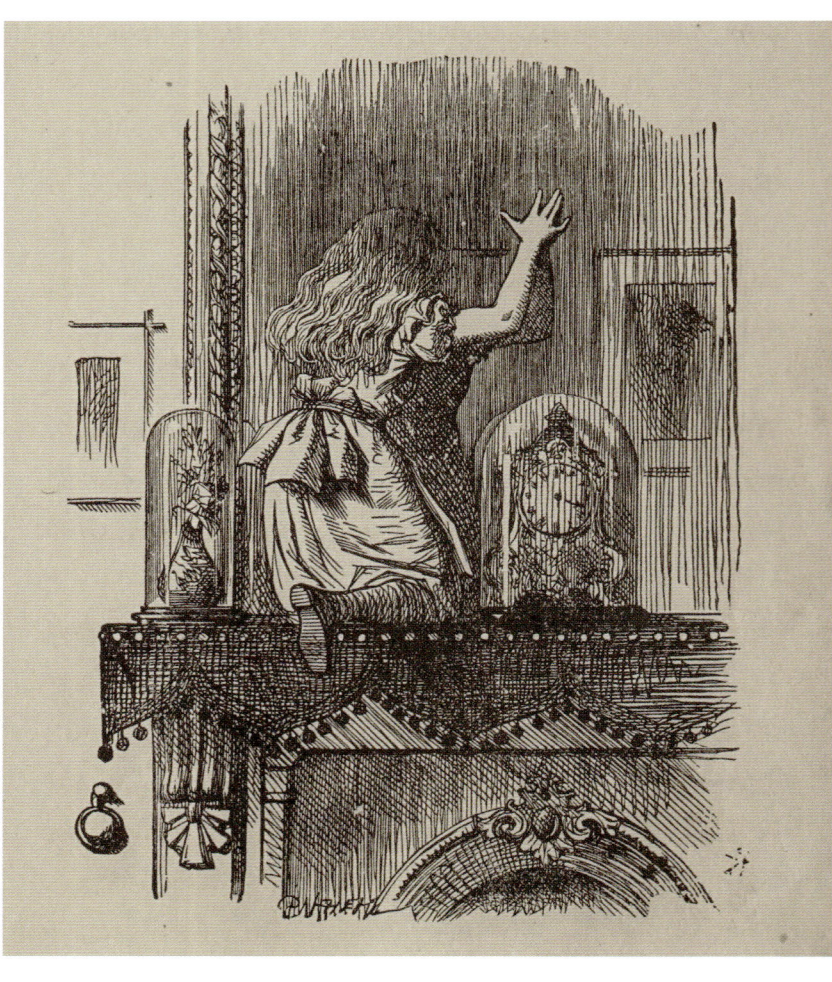

John Tenniel, *The Mirror on the Mantel*, wood engraving,
Lewis Carroll, *Through the Looking-Glass*, 1871.
Courtesy of the Library of Congress.

B IS FOR BOA CONSTRICTOR

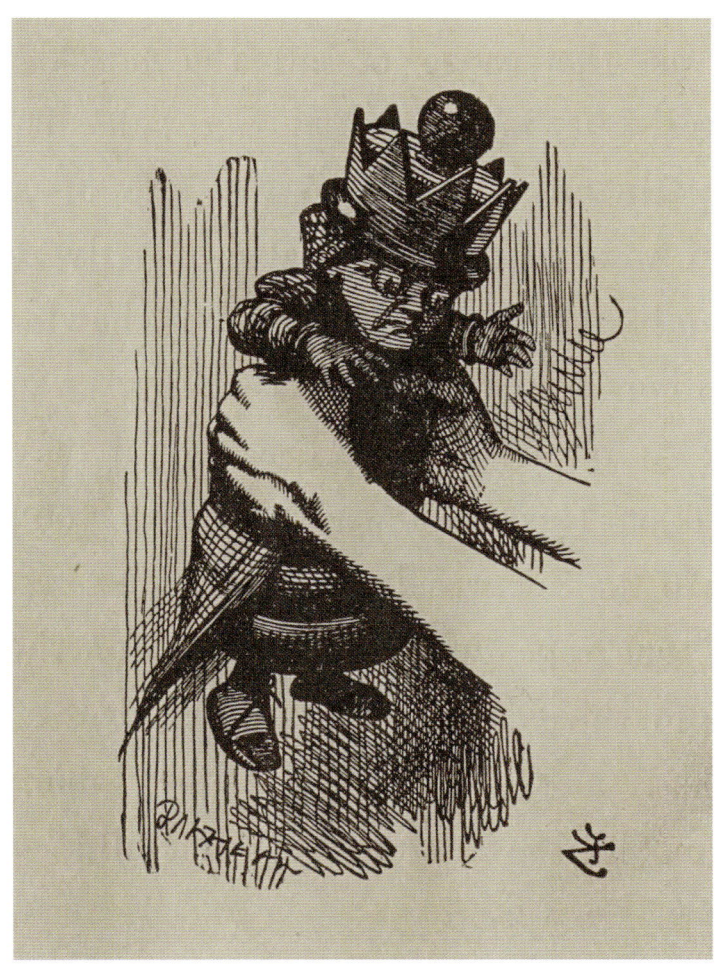

John Tenniel, *Shaking the Red Queen*, wood engraving,
Lewis Carroll, *Through the Looking-Glass*, 1871.
Courtesy of the Library of Congress.

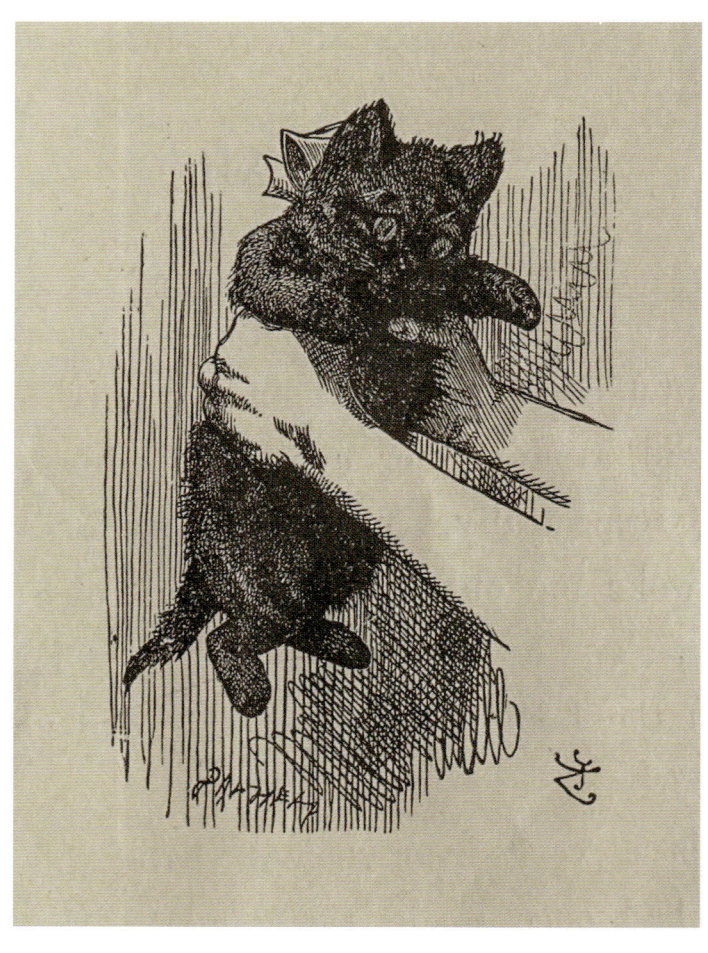

John Tenniel, *Shaking the Black Kitten*, wood engraving,
Lewis Carroll, *Through the Looking-Glass*, 1871.
Courtesy of the Library of Congress.

B IS FOR BOA CONSTRICTOR

dismissed as absurd or meaningless, but this description misses the fundamental point.

Dreams transcend the manifest world by transfiguring reality —by giving things a new form. This seemingly simple activity— the stuff of children's books—is, in fact, the grounds of our world-making capacity: our ability to envisage the world anew. These visions contain a transformative power that sustains our sense of vitality and helps us make sense of our experiences, integrating us into the larger social imaginary. Dreams are also the source of our ability to bring new worlds into existence, allowing us to survive the inevitable losses that we all must face.

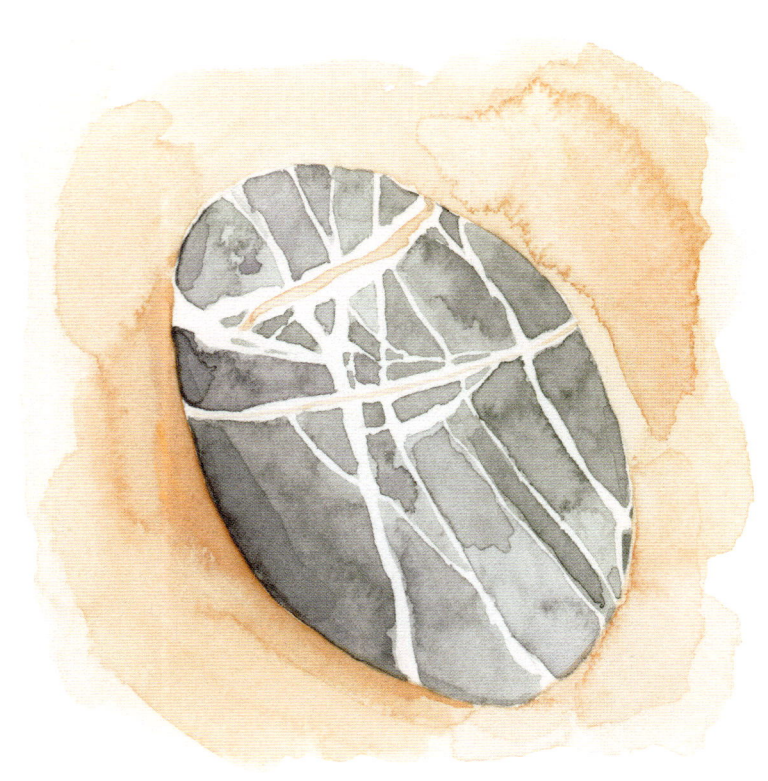

C IS FOR CANCER

On Labor Day 1978, during a regular monthly self-examination, the writer and activist Audre Lorde discovered a lump in her right breast. The tumor proved to be malignant. As Lorde processed the events that followed—diagnosis, hospitalization, and radical mastectomy—she careened through a series of emotional states, including pain, despair, fury, and sadness. Sometimes she felt as if she had no choice in the way these emotions washed over her. At other times, she felt her only choice was oblivion—"or a passivity that is very close to oblivion"—which, for the poet, was no choice at all.[1]

One of the activities that helped Lorde metabolize her experience was writing. The poet documented her physical and emotional experiences of the diagnosis and treatment as well as the punishing medical culture that surrounded breast cancer at the time. This remarkable testament was eventually published in 1980 in a book called *The Cancer Journals*.

Lorde's effort to document and examine her experience with cancer led to an unexpected outcome: she began to feel that "in the process of losing a breast I had become a more whole person."[2] Her record of this transformation retains its capacity to astonish readers more than forty years after its initial publication. It is a raw account of how a self-described "Black lesbian feminist mother lover poet" not only recovered from her physical illness but remade herself in the process. The book contains a powerful thesis about change. Radical transformation can be achieved, the poet suggests, by looking inward and by giving voice to what one finds there, whether grief, anger, pain, or sadness.

One of the key tools that Lorde relied on in this transformation was her dream life. Detailed reports of her dreams—as well as notes about the regularity of their comings and goings—punctuate *The Cancer Journals* like a heartbeat, serving as a steady companion to this testament of a transformation. Lorde describes, for instance, her recovery routine during the immediate aftermath of the mastectomy. She would sleep a few hours, wake up, "go to the john, write down my dreams on little scraps of paper without my glasses, take two aspirin, do my hand exercises, spider-crawling up the wall of the bathroom, and then go back to bed for another few hours and some more dreams."[3]

On other occasions, Lorde turned to her dreams as a means to reckon with the other losses that the mastectomy summoned. The night before her surgery, she dreamed of one of her earliest lovers, Eudora—not the first woman with whom she shared "body warmth and wildness" but the first who "totally engaged" her in loving. Lorde describes how Eudora came to her in a dream in all her lanky, snapdragon self, complete with a gap-toothed lopsided smile, and they simply sat, holding hands for a little while. The dream recalled the spring they spent in Mexico together, the night Eudora finally shared the pain of her own mastectomy, and the hesitation and tenderness Lorde felt as she touched the deeply scarred hollow under Eudora's shoulder. At the time, Lorde was nineteen years old. When she woke on the gray morning before her own surgery on September 22, 1978, Lorde was forty-four, Eudora was gone, and the poet wept, not out of fear for what she faced but out of deep feeling for her former lover.

Readers who are familiar with Lorde's writing might not be surprised at the central role that dreams play in *The Cancer Journals* and at her repeated insistence on the importance of attending these visions. Dreams are woven throughout the entirety of the poet's work. Her essay "Notes from a Trip to Russia" opens with a dream about going to a hospital in Moscow and includes the startling realization that "medicine and doctor's bills and all the rest of that are free."[4] (Access to health care was one of Lorde's ongoing concerns.)

Dreams also play a central role in the poet's most celebrated essay, "Poetry Is Not a Luxury." In this essay, Lorde makes one of her most powerful cases for living an examined life: "The quality of light by which we scrutinize our lives has direct bearing upon the product which we live, and upon the changes which we hope to bring about through those lives." For Lorde, dreams were crucial vehicles that helped her express the inexpressible. In this respect, they were natural allies to her poetic practice, offering a means to access nascent feelings and providing a spawning ground for daring new ideas. She describes dreams as "a safe-house for that difference so necessary to change and the conceptualization of meaningful action" and admits that she could immediately name at least ten ideas that she would have found "intolerable or incomprehensible and frightening, except that they came after dreams."[5] For Lorde, dreams were a crucial means to access the most difficult of truths, a kind of organic education guiding her through change.

At the heart of "Poetry Is Not a Luxury" is a call to develop a disciplined attention to dream life as means of self-examination and a method to care for the self. This radical proposal was almost immediately put to the test: the essay was published just one year before the poet was diagnosed with breast cancer. In this respect, *The Cancer Journals* can be read as a concrete deployment of the method Lorde proposes in her earlier essay—proof that a total transformation of being is possible through attending to the "intolerable, incomprehensible, and frightening" thoughts that come in dreams.

The last entry in Lorde's journal, dated July 10, 1980, is a dream report. The poet offers no interpretation of the vision, and none is needed. Lorde lets the dream stand as testament to her theory about the transformative power of attending to these visions:

7/10/80

I dreamt I had begun training to change my life, with a teacher who is very shadowy. I was not attending classes, but I was going to learn how to change my whole life, live differently, do everything in a new and different way. I didn't really understand, but I trusted the shadowy teacher. Another young woman who was there told me she was taking a course in "language crazure," the opposite of discrazure (the cracking and wearing away of rock). I thought it would be very exciting to study the formation and crack and composure of words, so I told my teacher I wanted to take that course. My teacher said okay, but it wasn't going to help me any because I had to learn something else, and I wouldn't get anything new from that class. I replied maybe not, but even though I knew all about rocks, for instance, I still liked studying their composition, and giving a name to the different ingredients of which they were made. It's very exciting to think of me being all the people in this dream.

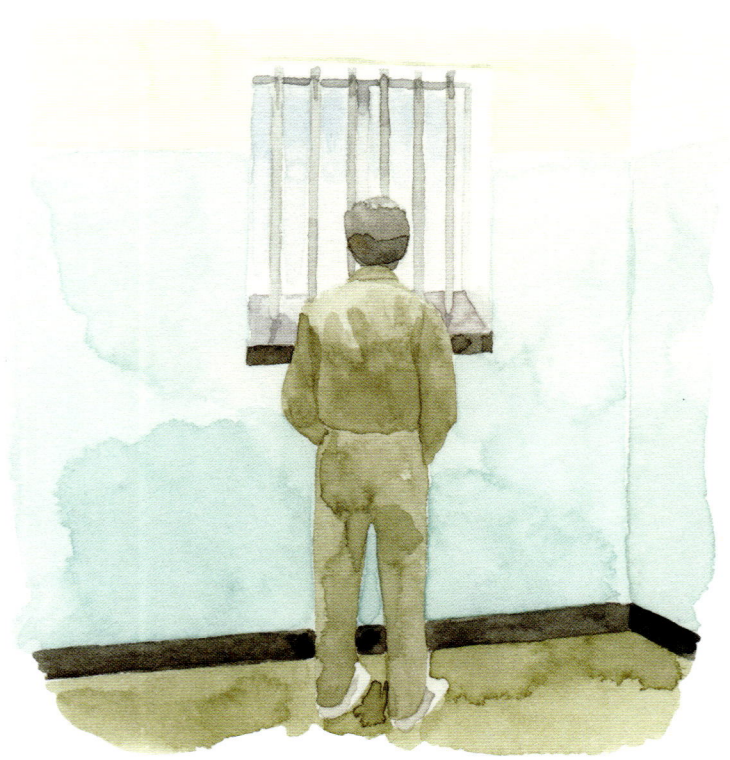

D IS FOR DEFENSE

I'll never forget the moment when I heard Nelson Mandela had died. I was browsing the shelves of an airport bookstore between flights in December 2013 and was perplexed to see bookstore employees setting up a display of the leader's autobiography, *Long Walk to Freedom*. The book had been published some twenty years prior, in 1994, the year Mandela became the first democratically elected president of South Africa. And then I saw a newspaper headline.

I bought a copy of Mandela's autobiography to keep me company on my long flight. The book begins, predictably enough, with the story of his childhood. Places and names are significant to his narrative. Born to the Thembu royal family, he was given the Xhosa forename Rolihlahla at his birth (which colloquially means "troublemaker"). When he was sent away to school at age seven, he acquired a clan name, Madiba (which continues to be used as a sign of respect and affection); a patrilineal grandfather provided his surname; and his first teacher, in accordance with colonial custom, gave him a Christian name, Nelson. After a rebellious youth, Mandela eventually made his way to the University of the Witwatersrand, where he slowly worked toward a degree (repeatedly failing his qualifying exams) as the only Black law student.

The basic outlines of what happened next are well known. As a young lawyer practicing in Johannesburg in the 1940s, he joined the African National Congress (ANC). In 1951, after the National Party took power, he helped organize the Defiance Campaign in response to the new apartheid laws. When the ANC's nonviolent tactics were met with violent reprisals from the Afrikaner-dominated government, Mandela began advocating for a different strategy. In 1961, he publicly stated, "If the government reaction is to crush by naked force our non-violent struggle, we will have to reconsider our tactics."[1] The young leader suffered a series of bans, served several jail sentences, and eventually cofounded the militant wing of the ANC, uMkhonto weSizme (MK) (Spear of the Nation). He went underground, undertook guerrilla warfare training, but eventually was captured and tried at the infamous Rivonia Trial, in which he and seven other ANC members were found guilty of a series of charges related to sabotage. Narrowly escaping the death penalty, Mandela was sentenced to life in prison on June 12, 1964. He did not see freedom again until February 11, 1990. After his release, he went on to lead the transitional government and became the first democratically elected president of South Africa, serving just one term from 1994 to 1999.

What enthralled me most about the autobiography was the section called "The Dark Years." The title refers to the years Mandela spent imprisoned on Robben Island. This part of the book reads like a training manual for surviving dark times. Madiba describes the various hardships imposed at the newly designed prison—a discriminatory dress code and segregated diet that the government created for each of the four racial groups it had invented ("black," "white," "coloured," and "Indian"), brutal forced labor at the island's lime quarry, and harsh restrictions on visitors and letters (one visitor and one letter were permitted every six months, always censored and often denied altogether). There is a sparse account of Mandela's devastation at the news of his mother's death in 1968. This grief was deepened less than a year later when he received a telegram informing him of his eldest son's death as a result of injuries sustained in a car crash. Each of these experiences imposed a distinct psychological pressure: "The challenge for every prisoner, particularly every political prisoner," Mandela counsels, "is how to survive prison intact, how to emerge from prison undiminished, how to conserve and even replenish one's beliefs."[2]

It was not, however, these soul-rending accounts or the leader's startling capacity for perseverance that brought me up short on that long flight. What jolted me awake was a nightmare that returned repeatedly to haunt Mandela during his twenty-seven-year imprisonment:

> I had one recurring nightmare. In the dream, I had just been released from prison—only it was not Robben Island, but a jail in Johannesburg. I walked outside the gates into the city and found no one there to meet me. In fact, there was no one there at all, no people, no cars, no taxis. I would then set out on foot toward Soweto. I walked for many hours before arriving in Orlando West, and then turned the corner toward 8115. Finally, I would see my home, but it turned out to be empty, a ghost house, with all the doors and windows open, but no one at all there.[3]

I can still remember my astonishment in coming across this passage. I was sitting on a plane, reading in the middle of the night, my book lit by a single overhead light. I felt seized by a powerful urge to wake the passenger sitting next to me so I could share the moment with someone. Mandela's nightmare seemed just as dramatic and important as his famous speech from the Rivonia Trial in which he named apartheid's injustice and defined the ideal for which he was prepared to die—a democratic and free society.[4] His nightmare seemed to attest to something similarly poignant about his experience of prison, offering both a private account of his emotional state and a profound testimony about the political conditions of his unfreedom.

The various locations mentioned in Mandela's dream can be traced back to sites of his lived experience—the first home he owned (the little red-brick house, number 8115 in Orlando West, a place Mandela once called the "center point" of his world, "the place marked with an X in my mental geography") and the jail in Johannesburg where he spent time awaiting trial in 1962 prior to the Rivonia Trial.[5] The nightmare also manages to index the tiny cell on Robben Island in which Mandela spent the majority of his sentence, albeit only through a negation: the dream prison "was *not* Robben Island," he insists. Such cancellations are a telltale sign of repression, a signal that something is being withheld from consciousness because of the pain that would come with its acknowledgment.[6]

A feature film based on the autobiography was released the same year Mandela died.[7] It opens with an adaptation of the leader's recuring nightmare. A bright white light fills the screen and slowly dissolves into a scene of neatly dressed children running excitedly into a little house to gather around a woman who is dispensing something from a plate. She laughs and waves at the children to be patient as she distributes the food. The camera pans around the bustling house and a deep voiceover begins: "I dream the same dream night after night. I am coming home to the house in Orlando. Everything is the way it was. They are all there, all the ones that I have loved most in the world. They seem fine, getting on with their lives. But they do not see me. They never see me."

Readers of the biography will recognize the scene takes place in number 8115 in Orlando West. But in the film version, Mandela's nightmare is turned inside out. Viewers witness a house that is full of laughter, as if life in the townships is carrying on just fine and no one misses his absence. In Mandela's own account of his nightmare, the world he emerges into is impoverished, emptied of all human presence, and his beloved home has been turned into a ghost house. The film's version manages to convey a sense of what it feels like to be denied the dimension of the human condition that involves belonging to a shared gaze—*to see and to be seen to exist*. But it also empties Mandela's nightmare of its political potency—the sense of unfreedom that the prolonged incarceration inflicts and that the nightmare manages to both represent and transfigure. Freedom to wander in an empty, uninhabited world is no freedom at all. What the film's version misses is the way the nightmare draws directly from Mandela's experience of apartheid, the way the dream *figures* the experience of being severed from human society.

This severing was particularly extreme in the first few years of Mandela's prison sentence when he was allowed to receive only one visitor and one letter every six months, but the process of his political isolation began long before his actual incarceration. In 1952, Mandela was among a group of leaders who were banned by the Afrikaner government through its Suppression of Communism Act. Although this act specifically targeted Communists, it was worded broadly, allowing it to include "any activity that allegedly promoted social, political, or economic change in South Africa." The banning aimed, in the short term, to prevent a variety of political figures from attending the national conferences of their respective parties. It was the first of a long series of bans that Mandela faced in the decade prior to his imprisonment.

People who were banned in apartheid South Africa had their movements severely restricted. Mandela was rarely allowed to leave his district of Johannesburg. He also was prevented from attending meetings of all kinds, not just political ones. He was prohibited, for instance, from attending his children's birthday parties or from speaking to more than one person at a time (both of which he defied the law to do). Banning was a kind of "walking imprisonment," and the strategy was one of the government's systematic attempts to immobilize leaders of groups who were resisting apartheid.

Whereas banning a particular political organization is a common government practice in modern history, the National Party's policy of banning individuals was unique among nations. Not since the Middle Ages had a political government openly attempted to formalize this kind of juridical outlawry. In addition to adapting to physical restrictions, banned persons were forced to resign from any offices they held in any organization, and they were prohibited from speaking publicly or from writing for any publication. Banned people could not be quoted, and their photographs were prohibited from being circulated.

Shortly before Mandela was due to be released in 1990, *Time* magazine produced a painting of the leader on its cover because no photographs of the freedom fighter had been taken since the early 1960s. No one knew what the man looked like after decades of imprisonment. As *Time*'s editor Robert L. Miller asked, "How do you capture the face of a man who has not been seen in public for the past 27 years?" His answer was to ask the artist Paul Davis to reimagine a portrait based on an earlier commission. (Four years prior, Davis had been asked to paint a portrait of the leader as a young man based on early photographs.) The magazine faxed a copy of the new portrait to Winnie Mandela for suggestions. The painter casually remarked that the process "was like the way police artists work."[8]

Banned individuals were also denied legal safeguards in the event of disappearance or death. In effect, banning represents an organized political attempt to expunge people from all aspects of social and public life, a gesture that seeks to deprive them of the usual entitlements and protections of human society. Mandela described this political act as an impingement of spirit: "Banning not only confines one physically, it imprisons one's spirit. It induces a kind of psychological claustrophobia that makes one yearn not only for freedom of movement but spiritual escape."[9]

Political theorists have analyzed the structural force of this kind of sovereign violence, but Mandela's dream offers a way to understand someone's lived experience of it. The nightmare is a visual correlate of the emotional experience of having one's personhood scraped away. All dreams are both visual documents and transfigurations of lived experience in this respect—mental representations that allow dreamers to work through their social position. This nightmare allowed Mandela to render in figurative terms the social and psychological impacts of the political violence he faced.

In the nightmare, Johannesburg is devoid of all people and cars, and Mandela's home is turned into a ghost house. This empty landscape can be understood as a dramatic presentation of the experience of being banned. The nightmare gave form to the violence that imprisonment enacts and the violence that apartheid enacts: the dream figuratively conveyed the pain of depriving a human being access to the human world. To translate into political language, the dream testifies to the way apartheid transforms the world into a ghost town.

But the nightmare also works like a protective shield, an intimate kind of defense against these political attacks on the leader's existence. This is necessary because these attacks do not only target the political body; they also aim to destroy psychic integrity. Dreams, Mandela intuitively understood, offer a means to protect oneself from this form of aggression. The dream's symbolic transformations preserve the mind's agency, in part by generating what Didier Anzieu calls a "psychical wrapping"—a secondary, protective skin for thought.[10]

Mandela's nightmare opened an interior landscape in which he found space to represent the terms of his political condition rather than be directly equated with it. This vision served as a kind of internal shield, helping to sustain his sense of self by turning this oppression into a figure of thought. Or to use Mandela's own terms, the dream helped him defend himself against that dimension of political violence that aimed to "imprison his spirit." This singular example shows how, in dark times, dream life can be our most intimate mode of civil defense.[11]

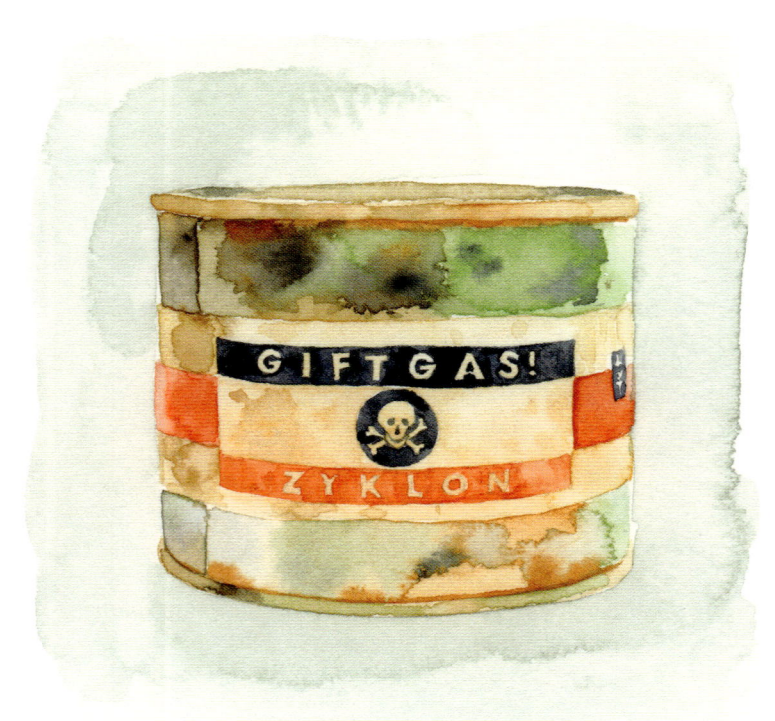

E IS FOR EVIL

In the late 1970s, the American psychiatrist Robert Jay Lifton conducted a study of Nazi doctors. By this point in this career, Lifton was already well known for his psychological studies of political violence. He had worked with survivors of the bombing of Hiroshima and with veterans who were organizing against the Vietnam War. He even gave testimony at the "Winter Soldier Investigation," an event that aimed to reveal a direct relationship between US military policy and war crimes in Vietnam.

In his memoir, Lifton notes that his study of Nazi doctors was different because his research involved investigating what he termed the "psychological and historical currents conducive to evil."[1] The psychiatrist's use of the term *evil* was considered and deliberate. Setting aside religious connotations, Lifton argues that evil is a specifically human phenomenon and the Nazi doctors provided one of its clearest examples. He felt compelled to study this group because they bore much of the responsibility for "the murderous ecology of Auschwitz." In his mind, there was no better word to evoke the extreme transgression that produced such extensive death and suffering, and as a psychiatrist, he felt it was his duty to try to understand the psychological machinations that produced this mentality. (Lifton did not reserve this judgment solely for Nazi doctors; he also described the American bombings of Hiroshima and Nagasaki as evil.)

With the help of a German colleague, Lifton was able to conduct interviews with twenty-nine men who had been directly involved with Nazi medicine at the highest levels. Twenty-eight of these men were doctors; one was a pharmacist. Most of the men in this group had worked in the concentration camps or had some association with Aktion T4, the Nazi program of medical euthanasia. Lifton was preoccupied by the question of how physicians—people who were otherwise committed by oath to do no harm—could become killers and how a genocide could be undertaken under the pretense of medical legitimacy.

Lifton's conclusion is complex: human nature, he argued, is not inherently cruel. In most cases, causing harm to another human being has profound psychological consequences for the perpetrator. It is only rare sociopaths who can participate in atrocities without experiencing lasting emotional impairment. But Lifton did find evidence of another, equally disturbing psychological truth: participation in mass murder need not require the presence of evil emotions or evil intention. In certain conditions—what he calls "atrocity-producing situations"—ordinary people will commit otherwise unthinkable acts.

For Lifton, the Nazi doctors were not faceless bureaucratic cogs. The perpetrators were aware of and responsible for their actions, even if they relegated this awareness to a remote region of their minds. His self-appointed task involved identifying the specific psychological traits that, when combined with the Nazi Party's ideological vision, enabled these doctors to carry out their genocidal work.

The Nazi Party's turn to medical killing was partly a response to complications arising from its face-to-face program of murder, which was carried out largely by the *Einsatzgruppen*, a paramilitary death squad whose members shot at close range some two million civilians between 1941 and 1945—Jewish people chiefly, but also Romani, Russian and Polish intelligentsia, "homosexuals," and others. Lifton interviewed a former German psychiatrist who had treated large numbers of *Einsatzgruppen* personnel, and the doctor reported that some 20 percent of these soldiers experienced symptoms of psychological decompensation—the radical disintegration of the personality that occurs when normal coping mechanisms fail. Lifton reports that many of these men experienced a sense of guilt in their dreams, which was often figured through various forms of punishment or retribution.[2] This all-too-human response—profound mental disturbance in the face of mass atrocity—is what induced the Nazis to seek a more "surgical" method of killing.

To my mind, this is some of the strongest evidence we have for the vital importance of dream life. These nighttime visions became a site where Nazi soldiers (and doctors, too, as we will see) were forced to encounter the emotional truth of their actions. The sense of guilt suggests there was an awareness—however fragile and subject to repression—of wrongdoing. In the context of a "atrocity-producing situation," dreams function as a kind of internal signal, imploring the dreamers to attend to what they know to be true and demanding an engagement with the emotional consequences of their actions. In their dream life, the killers encountered a powerful exhortation that was in direct conflict with the ideological world in which these men were commanded to kill. If only they had listened.

Lifton found similar evidence for the role of dreams among the Nazi doctors. One his interviewees included Dr. Horst D, who had worked at one of the Nazi killing centers for about a year. At the time of the interview in the 1970s, Dr. D was involved in complex legal proceedings. He was one of the few doctors who were investigated after the war. (The Nazi doctors were largely protected in postwar German society, often entering private practice with the consent of the medical profession.)[3] Lifton describes Dr. D as a "bearded vigorous man in his early sixties" who was "tense, cautious, and limited in his capacity to express feelings—wishing very much to explain himself and at the same time conflicted about his own explanation."[4]

Dr. D had been pressed into military service in 1940 before he was able to complete his medical thesis. He was quickly recruited to the Aktion T4 program by two professors of psychiatry who brought Dr. D to Berlin to attend a conference that was meant to convince recruits of the medical necessity of euthanasia. The professors made their case by leaning heavily on a 1920 legal treatise called "The Permission to Destroy Life Unworthy of Life," coauthored by a psychiatrist and a jurist. The Berlin conference presented doctors with the argument that euthanasia was "healing work" that was necessary to cure the ailing German society. This argument proved to be convincing to Dr. D, who felt a strong sense of duty to serve the senior members of his profession.

As Lifton makes clear throughout his sprawling study, this lethal combination of biomedical ideology, eugenic fantasy, and sense of duty to the profession came together to form the atrocity-producing situation. Nazi doctors felt duty bound to kill *in the name of medicine*. Mass murder became ideologically positioned as a therapeutic imperative. Genocide was required to remove a "diseased appendage from body of mankind."

After the Aktion T4 conference, Dr. D thought he would be joining a professional medical institution where he would carry out the "special treatment" with "patients" assigned to individual rooms. The reality was murder on a mass scale. The "patients" were largely Jewish and Romani civilians who arrived on trains and buses. "Selections" were made at the arrivals ramp, dividing those who were fit for labor from those who were immediately sent to the gas chambers. Dr. D's role was to look over the charts, decide on a fictive cause of death, and supervise the process of murder.

When Lifton queried Dr. D about whether he was directly responsible for releasing the Zyklon B gas into the death chambers, he became angry, answering with a defensive retort: "What does this have to do with psychological matters?" Lifton reports that the doctor eventually calmed down but never directly answered the question, only admitting that it was his role to determine whether the gas had been "effective."

Despite his limited capacity to express emotion, Dr. D did communicate some conflicted feelings about his work. While many of his "patients" arrived in a "hopeless condition," he admitted that, at times, he was able to make an attachment to some of them, and he conceded that it "might have happened" that he felt some sympathy for them.

This sympathy and resulting sense of guilt manifest in Dr. D's dreams. He told Lifton about one of these visions: "I can still see before me . . . one group of people . . . [and] I thought I should have saved them, that I should have helped them." During the interview, Dr. D associated this dream-vision with an actual group of people who had arrived at the killing center from far away: "I don't know who judged them," he reported, implying that they had been wrongly "selected" for euthanasia. After this startling admission, Dr. D paused and then added, with quiet agitation: "This is getting dangerous. . . . Saying that from a standpoint of lawyers means that I have guilt feelings. . . . What I just said could mean the death penalty to me."[5]

It is hard to overstate the significance of this admission. Extraordinarily few Nazis ever acknowledged any wrongdoing or assumed responsibility for the evil acts they committed. The one thing that brought one of these perpetrators to face his responsibility and to utter it aloud was a dream.

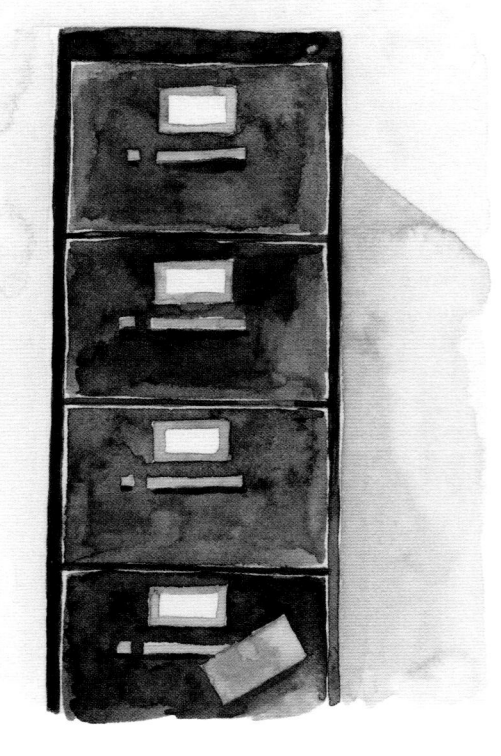

F IS FOR FILING CABINET

For more than a year, Abigail Echo-Hawk dreamed of a filing cabinet—a standard, black, filing cabinet that was completely unremarkable apart from a purple sticker that was visible on the bottom drawer. When she saw the filing cabinet in her dreams, Abigail always felt a strong inner command to quiet herself, a kind of silent instruction to listen. And once she had achieved the required state of quietude in the dream, she could hear women softly weeping.

When the dream started to recur, Abigail consulted people in her community. Echo-Hawk is a member of the Kitkehahki band of the Pawnee Nation of Oklahoma, born and raised in Alaska among the upper Ahtna Athabascan people of Mentasta Lake. From a young age, she was taught that when a dream recurs, it means the ancestors are talking to you. It might be Creator, or it might be your kin, but you had better pay attention.

Abigail consulted her family, her elders and aunties, and her broader community. At the time, she was working at Washington State University developing policy about how to conduct health research in ways that respect tribal sovereignty. No one in her community had any ideas about what the dream might be about. At night, when Abigail closed her eyes, she continued to be visited by the image of the filing cabinet, felt the need to quiet herself, and heard the women weeping.

Life carried on. Her academic career flourished. Washington State has one of the largest centers on American Indian and Alaska Native research in the country. But Abigail struggled with the institution's entrenched colonialism: "They wanted me to look Indian. They wanted me to say Indian things, but they didn't actually want me to act like one. They didn't want me grounded in culture and tradition. I remember once having a fight about including a prayer at an opening event. I thought—*come on*, of course we need to have a prayer. It's cultural protocol."[1]

Abigail similarly struggled when it came to conducting research in the academic context. For one grant she participated in, the lead researchers told her she needed to take off her "Native hat" and put on her researcher hat. Abigail reflects: "I thought, you're asking me to remove a piece of myself—actually, all of myself." (Like many Indigenous peoples of the Americas, Abigail uses the terms *Native*, *Indian*, and *Indigenous* interchangeably.)

One day the CEO of the Seattle Indian Health Board (SIHB) approached Abigail to ask her to consider joining the organization. The SIHB is a federally qualified health center in Seattle that provides primary medical and cultural services—or what Abigail simply calls "love and care"—to the urban Indigenous community. The health board also has a research wing called the Urban Indian Health Institute (UIHI), which is one of twelve Tribal Epidemiology Centers (TECs) across the United States working to represent Indigenous people in health research, data analysis, and evaluation. The institute is the only such center that focuses on the nation's urban Indigenous population, which is the majority of the Indigenous population. Approximately 75 percent of American Indian and Alaska Native people live in urban settings.

The idea of working in an environment where Abigail could "be Native 100% of the time" was enticing. There would be no more code switching. She would be surrounded by a largely Indigenous staff. Following cultural protocols would not be questioned but instead joyfully celebrated. But Abigail was not looking for another job. For the first time in her life, she was being paid well, and despite the difficulties of the university environment, she had job security and was being courted for leadership roles in the academy. As she considered the offer, she consulted her family, she prayed, and she asked for guidance from her community. The decision was eventually made collectively: she would leave the university to join the Urban Indian Health Institute.

When she walked into her new office on her first day, Abigail was still unsure. Was it the right decision to walk away from all that she had painstakingly built in her role at the university? "I was actually feeling really scared. But when I walked into my office, I saw something out of the corner of my eye, and I realized I had made the right choice."

In the corner of her new office was a black filing cabinet with a purple sticker on the bottom drawer. Abigail was not so much surprised as reassured. Now she understood where her ancestors were guiding her. As it turned out, the drawer with the purple sticker contained the testimonies of 148 Native women from the Seattle area. The testimonies had been collected years prior, but at the time, a decision was made ("by men!" Abigail emphasizes) to file the information for fear of the upset it might cause if it were made public. And so the testimonies were buried in the black filing cabinet and all but forgotten. Abigail immediately knew that these were the voices she had been hearing in her dream. And she knew that it was her sacred responsibility to find a way to make these voices heard.

In 2018, together with her team at UIHI, Abigail released the first in a series of reports about what these testimonies revealed.[2] The statistics were shattering: of the 148 urban Native women who were interviewed, 139 (a staggering 94 percent) had been raped or sexually coerced at some point in their lives, and a majority of the 139 (73 percent) had been victims of street harassment. Many of the women who were raped or coerced did not report the crimes to police. Of those who did seek justice, only 8 percent of charges ended in a conviction. Over half of the women had experienced some form of homelessness, and 42 percent had attempted suicide.

Later in 2018, Abigail led new research resulting in a second report detailing the missing and murdered Indigenous women and girls (MMIWG) crisis across the country. The report highlighted the disproportionate number of cases in urban areas and found a further 153 cases that did not exist in law enforcement records. The report also drew attention to the difficulties encountered in obtaining MMIWG data and information. Of the 5,712 cases of MMIWG reported in 2016, only 116 were logged in the US Department of Justice's federal missing persons database.

Systematic racism, underreporting, racial misclassification, and ongoing distrust of law enforcement have meant that the numbers in these ground-breaking reports likely underestimate the true extent of violence. As Abigail says in one of UIHI's reports, "Missing and murdered Indigenous women and girls (MMIWG) is not a new crisis in the United States. This continuous and pervasive assault on our matriarchs has existed since colonizers set foot on this land. Decades of advocacy and activism fell on deaf ears, while more and more of our women went missing and were murdered."[3]

Police and other agents of the colonial state are intent on seeing Indigenous people through a particular lens, a kind of a bureaucratic gaze that refuses to recognize what is given to be seen. These punishing forms of misrecognition have constrained the perceptibility of Indigenous life.[4]

Dreams offer another way of seeing and a different mode of listening. Since UIHI's release of the reports built from the testimonies that Abigail discovered in the black filing cabinet, the attention around the MMIWG crisis has grown exponentially. Thousands of news articles have been published highlighting the information revealed in the reports. Legislators, government agencies, and the media have been forced to pay attention. Numerous state and federal bills have been drafted, introduced, or passed that address issues related to the crisis.

The most radical ideas often come from groups of people who have been forced to confront systems of oppression. It may be that the dominant Western paradigms of knowledge will never accept dreams as a vital source of knowledge. This does not matter, for dream we do. And those who attend these revelatory distillations of experience will always have the means to see beyond what is given to sight, accessing the worlds not yet born and envisioning a future in the present.

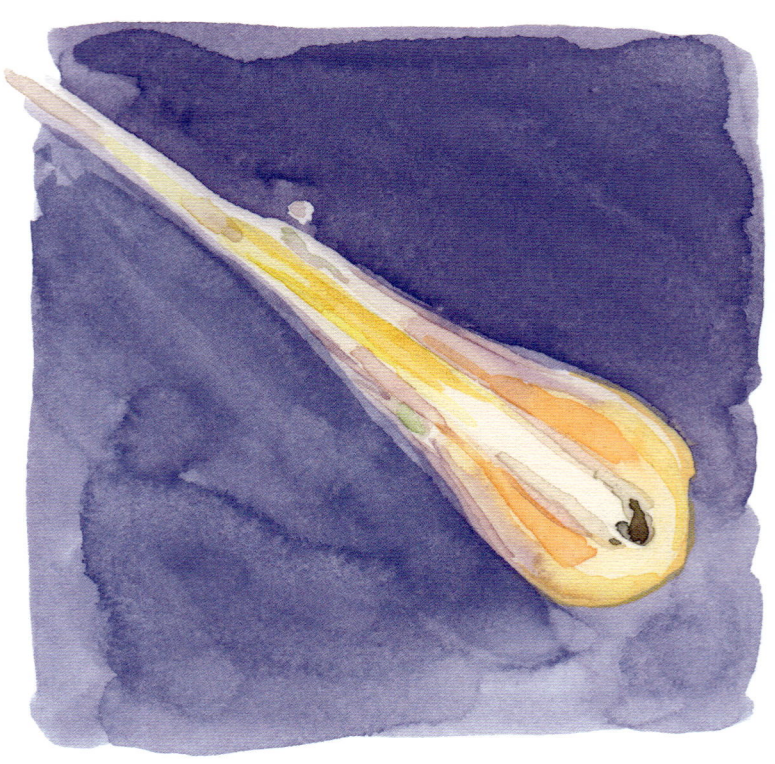

G IS FOR GRIEF

One of the oldest dreams in the historical record dates back more than four thousand years. The dream was set down in the writing system of ancient Mesopotamia—cuneiform, named for its wedge-shaped signs. The clay tablets on which the dream was recorded were uncovered in 1849, when a team of archeologists excavated the ruins of an ancient library in the city of Nineveh, a site that lies within the borders of modern-day Iraq.

By all accounts, the Royal Library of Ashurbanipal was magnificent in its day, containing some thirty thousand texts and clay tablets from various places, many of which ended up in the British Museum. (After Iraq gained independence in the 1930s, the country introduced laws regulating the export of antiquities, but by then, many artifacts had been excavated and shipped to London.) In the decades after these tablets were acquired by the British Museum (some would say stolen), historians began piecing together story fragments that they eventually realized belonged to a single, sprawling poem—what we now know as the *Epic of Gilgamesh*. The story is a remarkable mix of wild adventure and anguished tragedy. It also contains one of the oldest articulations of that wonderfully modern expression: love is love.

The Nineveh tablets containing the poem are thought to have been inscribed by a scholar-priest named Sîn-leqi-unnenni, who probably collected several versions of the story to form the epic in the eleventh century BCE. (Like Homer, Sîn-leqi-unnenni might have been a real person, or he might be a literary invention.) But the first mention of Gilgamesh's name dates to 2100 BCE, which means that this story predates both the earliest editions of the Bible and Homer's *Odyssey* by more than a thousand years.

The story chronicles the adventures of King Gilgamesh, the powerful ruler of Uruk, an ancient city located on a channel of the Euphrates River. Like all great epics, it is a story of transformation—how a ruler with a restless heart finally achieves self-understanding but also how this process of transformation brings a measure of peace to his city. Along the way, readers get lost with the protagonist in magical forests, are swept away on deadly seas, and even descend into the underworld. The cast includes scorpion people, a bull the size of a city, and a wise woman who runs an alehouse.

The story begins with a narrator urging readers to travel to the magnificent city of Uruk and look for the cedarwood box hidden in the foundations of the city:

> Undo its lock of bronze,
> open the door to its secrets,
> take up the tablet of lapis lazuli and read aloud:
>
> read of all that Gilgamesh went through,
> read of all his suffering.[1]

The story's compelling framing narrative embeds readers as active agents in the story as if the narrator has handed responsibility to us as the newest keepers of the tale.

When we first meet Gilgamesh, he is "great, magnificent, and terrible!" Part human and part god, the king is known for using his extraordinary strength to obtain what he wants. Eighteen feet tall and six feet wide, he physically oppresses men and "lets no bride go home to her groom," sexually violating the women of Uruk as he pleases.

It should be noted here that the *Epic of Gilgamesh* was composed by men and for men.[2] In ancient Mesopotamia, women could own and inherit property, divorce their husbands, run a business, bring lawsuits, and so on, but it is not clear how much access they had to education and politics. Even though women characters take a backseat in the *Epic*, they play a central role at major turning points in the narrative. And unlike in the classical tradition, where women often paid a high price for speaking in the public sphere (think of Cassandra, who was given a gift of foresight but cursed to never to be believed), women in the *Epic of Gilgamesh* are portrayed as the bearers of a special kind of knowledge, a deeper, nonrational wisdom that remains largely unavailable to men.

At the beginning of the story, women of the city beg the gods for help against Gilgamesh's tyranny. Hearing their complaints, the gods respond by creating the hero—Enkidu, "a son of silence" who knows no people or country and whose body is covered with fur. Enkidu grows up among a herd of gazelles that he protects from the hunter's traps. Consistently described as "gentle," Enkidu is eventually tamed by the priestess Shamhat, who introduces him to the human world by granting him access to her body.

In some translations, Shamhat is described as a sex worker or a "harlot," but she is employed by the temple, and in other parts of the story, she performs important religious rituals. Shamhat's wisdom is closely connected to her sexuality. As Audre Lorde might have said, she is versed in the "uses of the erotic."[3] Shamhat not only has access to this special form of knowledge, but she also mobilizes it as a source of transformation: "She showed the wild man what women can do / and his lust wrapped him around her body." After six days and seven nights with Shamhat, Enkidu is tamed. Afterward, when he tries to return to his herd, the gazelles now run from him: "Enkidu had sullied his spotless body."[4] This is the earliest description we have of the revelation of sexual knowledge (predating the Genesis story of Adam and Eve by thousands of years). In this version, unlike in the Biblical account, Shamhat is rewarded for introducing this knowledge to Enkidu. Part of her role in the story is to prepare him to meet his beloved.

The priestess reveals to Enkidu that Gilgamesh has been dreaming of him. At this point, the narrative swings back to the protagonist Gilgamesh, who is also being readied to meet his match—in this case, through the vehicle of a dream. This is one of the earliest dreams ever recorded.

In the dream, Gilgamesh sees stars blazing in the sky, and when one falls to the ground like a meteorite, he tries to pick it up but cannot budge it. The people of Uruk flock to the fallen meteorite, and Gilgamesh wraps his arms around it, loving and embracing it "like a wife."[5] Then the king has a second dream, in which he sees a great ax lying in the marketplace. Once again, the people of Uruk gather around, flocking to the foreign object. This time, Gilgamesh is able to pick up the great ax and sets it at his mother's feet, again wrapping his arms around it and loving it "like a wife."

After waking from these dreams, Gilgamesh immediately consults his mother, the goddess Ninsun. And here we meet the second, striking female character in the story. The mighty queen Ninsun is repeatedly described as clever and wise, knowing everything. She has access to a special form of knowledge that includes the gift of foresight and an understanding of dreams. Ninsun knows her son's destiny, and after hearing his dream report, she declares, "My son, the ax you saw is a man. / You will wrap your arms around him / and love him like a wife, / and I will declare him your equal."[6] The poignancy of this exchange is hard to miss. One of the earliest recorded dreams involves learning how to recognize your beloved when he finally appears and how to simply "love him and let him love you," as James Baldwin might have put it.[7]

The rest of the story follows from this powerful revelation of love: the queen's prophecy comes true, and Enkidu comes to Uruk, although at first as Gilgamesh's rival. The two men meet when Enkidu blocks Gilgamesh's path into the house where a wedding is taking place. The wild man is resolute about preventing the king from raping any more of Uruk's women, and the two men begin to brawl, butting like bulls. But Gilgamesh quickly comes to recognize his foe as the comrade promised to him in his dreams. In short order, the two men embrace and become inseparable. Gilgamesh's mother, Ninsun, formally adopts Enkidu as a son, and the pair go on many adventures, including a journey to the cedar forest to battle the fierce monster Humbaba, the great forest guardian who preys on the people of Uruk.

After a pitched battle, the two men kill the monster and return to Uruk on a cedar raft, triumphantly bearing Humbaba's head. Once home, Gilgamesh washes his hair, cleans his gear, and puts on a clean cloak. When he dons his crown, the goddess Ishtar catches sight of his beauty and immediately proposes: "Come, Gilgamesh! Marry me, / give me the fruit of your body!" But Gilgamesh recalls the fates suffered by each of Ishtar's former lovers, and he rebuffs her. Enraged, the goddess rushes up to the heavens to persuade her father, Anu, to give her the fiery bull of heaven so that she can have her vengeance. Anu eventually grants his daughter's wish, and the bull of heaven causes havoc in Uruk until Gilgamesh and Enkidu discover its weak spot and kill it. They return to the palace for a great celebration.

That night, Enkidu has a dream in which he sees the gods gathering in an assembly. They feel that the two heroes have insulted them by killing the bull and decide that one of them must die. Enkidu realizes it will be him and wakes, delirious. He immediately goes to Gilgamesh with tears flowing like streams: "my fate is carved: some people die before their time."[8] Gilgamesh tries to calm his beloved, to no avail. Enkidu falls ill and grows weaker by the day. Within a fortnight, he is dead.

Gilgamesh is shattered by the loss of his beloved. He weeps for six days and seven nights, refusing to let the body be buried. Finally, after a maggot falls from Enkidu's nose, Gilgamesh relents and offers up a great lament and an impossibly lavish funeral. But his grief remains unbroken:

Hear me, young men, hear me!
Hear me, elders of vast Uruk, hear me!
I weep for my friend Enkidu,
I cry as bitterly as a weeper woman.

Ax at my side, strength of my arm,
Sword in my belt, shield in my hand!
My festival dress, my belt of joy!
An evil wind rose and robbed me of you.[9]

Unable to bear the loss, Gilgamesh spends the rest of the epic wandering the wilds with hollowed cheeks, a wrecked heart, and a mind full of grief. He sails the waters of death and even goes to the underworld in an effort to bring his companion back to life. But without his beloved, Gilgamesh can no longer accomplish fabulous deeds. He returns to Uruk empty handed but rich with that painful wisdom that comes from a great loss. The tale closes as it began, with a meditation on the city: "Climb the wall of Uruk. Walk its length. / Survey the foundation, study the brickwork . . ."[10]

If the *Epic of Gilgamesh* carries a teaching, it is that love is the ultimate transformative force. That might sound like the shallow sentimentalism of the romance genre, but in this tale, the force of love is more like James Baldwin's insight that our capacity to be undone by this experience is inextricably connected to and a necessary part of social change: "How do you live if you can't love? And how can you live if you do?"[11] Love, in this definition, is not simply a personal feeling but, as Baldwin put it, "a state of being, or a state of grace—not in the infantile American sense of being made happy but in the tough and universal sense of quest and daring and growth."[12] The *Epic of Gilgamesh* is one of the most profound articulations of this idea. When the story begins, Gilgamesh is authoring all manner of devastation. Tyranny, the story teaches us, is a symptom of lovelessness. Genuine social transformation requires the capacity to be broken and remade by love and its loss. The force of this experience, Gilgamesh's dream reveals, is like a blazing star that lands at your feet.

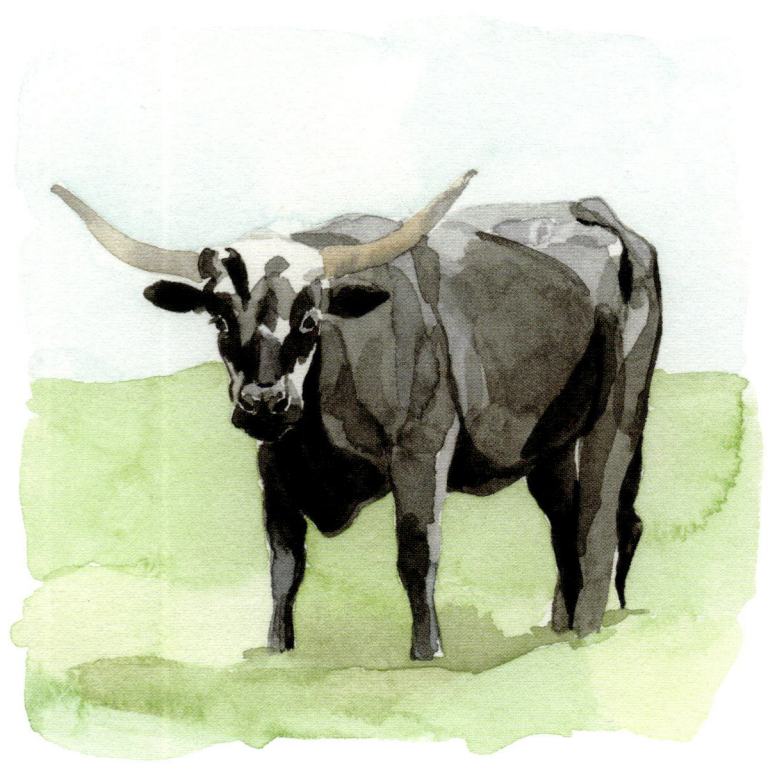

H IS FOR HOMEWORK

Perched high up in the hills of Antananarivo, the capital of Madagascar, is the Lycée Andohalo, a public secondary school built 1908 when the island was under French colonial control. When it was built and for a long time afterward, the lycée was the only public high school in the country. Perhaps more significantly, the country's First Republic was proclaimed in the school's amphitheater in 1958, and the new Malagasy national anthem was played there for the first time.

Madagascar's independence was hard won. Democratic political organizing began in 1945, but a more forceful effort began in March 1947, when a few hundred Malagasy revolutionaries attacked a French military base on the eastern side of the island. This area was where generations of Malagasy had been subject to forced labor on French plantations after a popular uprising was crushed by the French at the end of the nineteenth century. As this new rebellion spread, the response was swift and brutal. The French brought eighteen thousand troops to the island (most were African soldiers from Senegal who were conscripted by the French) and began experimenting with new "pacification" tactics—France's ugly euphemism for torture, rape, the torching of entire villages, and mass murder.

The number of Malagasy who were killed by French troops during the rebellion is a figure of some dispute, but by the time the uprising was brutally repressed in February 1949, the high commissioner of Madagascar reported to the French National Assembly that between 90,000 and 100,000 Malagasy had been killed.[1] France has never officially acknowledged or apologized for the violence it inflicted on Malagasy during this period of decolonization, and the memories of these events remain contentious to this day.[2]

One of the most unusual testimonies from this period is a collection of dreams written down by high school students attending the Lycée Andohalo. The students' teacher, Octave Mannoni, an expatriot Frenchman, collected the dream reports as part of a homework assignment.

Mannoni started teaching at the lycée in 1931, but in 1945, as soon as the Second World War ended, he took a six-month leave (an entitlement for all expatriate civil servants) to undergo psychoanalysis with Jacques Lacan in Paris. After his leave, Mannoni returned to Madagascar, resuming his position at the Lycée Andohalo for the school year 1947–48, a year that over-lapped with the rebellion. It was during this year that he issued the unusual dream homework assignment to his students.

The student's dreams offer remarkable testimonies about what has been called "one of the bloodiest episodes of colonial repression on the African continent."[3] But they are not straight-forward documents. These accounts survive in a book called *The Psychology of Colonization* that Mannoni published in 1950.

Mannoni quickly recognized the problematic nature of his own text, which, as its title indicates, attempts to provide a psychological analysis of what the author calls "the colonial situation." In a note added to the 1956 English edition, now retitled *Prospero and Caliban: The Psychology of Colonization*, Mannoni admits that he "rashly employed certain theoretical concepts which needed more careful handling than I realised at the time. I must frankly admit that I am now disturbed by the obvious weaknesses of the book."[4] This did not stop him from continuing to defend his central claim that the Malagasy (and all colonized peoples) suffer from a "dependency complex."

Prospero and Caliban is a classic example of epistemological violence. In this case, Mannoni uses Western psychological theories to pathologize his non-Western subjects, including his students, impose meaning on their experiences, and in the pro-cess impoverish and denigrate an existing (Malagasy) lifeworld by imposing another (Western) lifeworld in its place.

This violence is evident in Mannoni's handling of his students' dreams. In his book, each dream report is accompanied by an interpretation in which the images appearing in the dreams are assumed to stand for something else—meanings that Mannoni himself supplies. The fact that the dreams were written in a language foreign to the students (as part of their French homework) does not stop Mannoni from attaching great importance to word choice.

When one dreamer has a terrifying nightmare about climbing a tree to escape an angry black bull, Mannoni claims the tree "stands for the mother." When Senegalese soldiers appear in one of his student's dreams, Mannoni sees "the psychologically deeper image of the father." When a fourteen-year-old boy named Razafi dreams of Senegalese soldiers chasing him with rifles making a noise like galloping horses, Mannoni claims the images can be "explained by the fact that the child has witnessed the sexual act." And when a thirteen-year-old girl named Elphine dreams of being disemboweled by a fierce black ox whose head was "mottled with white," Mannoni claims it contains evidence of the Malagasy's "mutilation complex."[5]

By laying these invented meanings on top of the students' dream reports, Mannoni supplies the psychological evidence for his fallacious claim that "Malagasies' dreams faithfully reflect their overriding need for security and protection."[6] Mannoni's students offered a glimpse of the political terror that was happening across the French colony of Madagascar, but having born witness to this revelation, the colonizer shut his eyes to the truth of what he was shown.

The radical psychiatrist Frantz Fanon rightly called *Prospero and Caliban* a "dangerous" book. Fanon, whose articulation of the psychological force of colonial violence has been taken up around the globe, reproduced the Malagasy dreams in a chapter of his own book *Black Skins, White Masks*, called "The So-Called Dependency Complex of Colonized Peoples."[7] Fanon included the students' dreams but omitted Mannoni's interpretations, effectively excising the colonizer's imposition of meaning.

Rather than offer a counterinterpretation, Fanon provides political context for the dreams. He cites a report that appeared in an Antananarivo newspaper that included details about the torture being perpetuated on the local population by Senegalese soldiers acting on behalf of the French. By treating the dreams as containing their own evidence—as attestations to the situation of their gestation—Fanon offers a powerful instruction for how we should *attend* to dream life. His compact statement reads like a manifesto—a powerful call that dream life should be restored from the hands of colonial interpretation:

> What must be done is to restore this dream to its *proper time*, and this time is the period during which eighty thousand natives were killed—that is to say, one of every fifty persons in the population; and to its *proper place*, and this place is an island of four million people, at the center of which no real relationship can be established, where dissension breaks out in every direction, where the only masters are lies and demagogy. One must concede that in some circumstances the *socius* is more important than the individual.[8]

Dreams awaken the mind to the realities of the world. It is not an exaggeration to say that the way we choose to attend to these visions may well determine the fate of our souls.

Redacted pages from Octave Mannoni, *Prospero and Caliban: The Psychology of Colonization* (1950), 2nd ed., translated by Pamela Powesland (New York: Praeger, 1964).

H IS FOR HOMEWORK

EPILOGUE TO PART I – DREAMS

MALAGASIES' dreams faithfully reflect ████████████████████ ██████████████████ All the dreams quoted below were, it is true, recorded at a time of public disturbance, but their authors had seen nothing of the disorders and knew about them only from hearsay. The following nightmare, described by a twenty-three-year-old Merina cook,████████████████████████████████ ██ ███████

The cook's dream. 'I was being chased by an angry black bull. Terrified, I climbed up into a tree and stayed there till the danger was past. I came down again, trembling all over.'

████████████████████████████ ████████████████ ███████████████████████████████████ ███████leave no doubt ████████████████████████████ ███████████████████████████████████████ ███████████████████████████████████████ ████████the enemy ████████████████████the child can hide ███ ██████████

███████the figure of the Senegalese ██████████████ ██ ███████████████████

[1] There is a little-known Merina *Key to Dreams*, which is a mixture of symbolical interpretations and superstitions. Dreams about bulls have a prominent place in it. Being attacked by a bull is supposed to warn the dreamer that he is threatened by sorcery, the bull representing the sorcerer. If the dreamer is caught on the bull's horns it means that the spell will be effective and he must seek protective magic. The colour of the coat must be noted because it indicates the colouring of the originator of the sorcery.
██

89

Dream of a thirteen-year-old boy, Rahevi. 'While going for a walk in the woods, I met two black men. "Oh," I thought, "I am done for!" I tried to run away but couldn't. They barred my way and began jabbering in a strange tongue. I thought they were saying, "We'll show you what death is." I shivered with fright and begged, "Please, Sirs, let me go, I'm so frightened." One of them understood French but in spite of that they said, "We are going to take you to our chief." As we set off they made me go in front and they showed me their rifles. I was more frightened than ever, but before reaching their camp we had to cross a river. I dived deep into the water and thanks to my presence of mind found a rocky cave where I hid. When the two men had gone I ran back to my parents' house.'

Josette's dream. The dreamer, a young girl, got lost and sat down on a fallen tree-trunk. A woman in a white dress told her that she was in the midst of a band of robbers. The account goes on: '"I am a schoolgirl", I said, trembling, "and I lost my way here when I was going home from school," and she replied: "Follow this path, child, and you children will find your way home."'

Dream of a fourteen-year-old boy, Raȝafi. He is being chased by (Senegalese) soldiers who 'make a noise like galloping horses as they run', and 'show their rifles in front of them'. The dreamer escapes by becoming invisible; he climbs a stairway and finds the door of his home.

fear of the bull is associated with the image of the sorcerer.

Among the Malagasies the image of the mother (so far as I know) is never anything but protective,

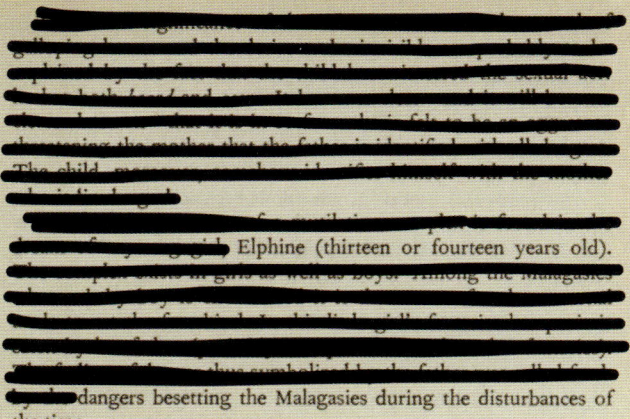

Elphine (thirteen or fourteen years old).

dangers besetting the Malagasies during the disturbances of the time.

Elphine's dream. 'I dreamed that a fierce black ox was chasing me. He was big and strong. On his head, which was almost mottled (*sic*) with white he had two long horns with sharp points. "Oh how dreadful," I thought. The path was getting narrower. What should I do? I perched myself in a mango-tree, but the ox rent its trunk. Alas, I fell among the bushes. Then he pressed his horns into me; my stomach fell out and he devoured it.'

Raza's dream. In his dream the boy heard someone say at school that the Senegalese were coming. 'I went out of the school yard to see.' The Senegalese were indeed coming. He ran home. 'But our house had been dispersed by them too.' 'Dispersed' is a mistake, owing to association with the idea of 'piercing' (compare above, the horns with which the ox rent the trunk of the mango-tree).

---

[2] The dreams from which those given here are drawn come from various sources, but in the main they have been collected in schools in the form of French homework. Those which appeared to be inventions have been eliminated, not because such fantasies are without interest but because their interpretation is more difficult. By contrast with the real dreams they were all very 'optimistic'.

███
███
███
███
███
██ a Malagasy family usually lives all together ████████████
█████████████████████████
███
███
███
███████████████████████████████

Dream of a fourteen-year-old boy, Si. 'I was walking in the garden and felt something like a shadow behind me. All around me the leaves were rustling and falling off, as if a robber was in hiding among them, waiting to catch me. Wherever I walked, up and down the alleys, the shadow still followed me. Suddenly I got frightened and started running, but the shadow took great strides and stretched out his huge hand to take hold of my clothes. I felt my shirt tearing, and screamed. My father jumped out of bed when he heard me scream and came over to look at me, but the big shadow had disappeared and I was no longer afraid.'

███
███
███
███
███
███
███
███
███
███
███
███
███████████████████ the children feel they are in danger
██████ their parents are afraid ███████████████████████
███████████████████████████████

Senegalese soldier (a fear which at the time was objectively justified). ██ ██ ███████████ external dangers. ████████████████████ ██ ████████████ evidence ██████████████ *the father is afraid,* ██ ██ ██ ████████ distress most commonly expressed.

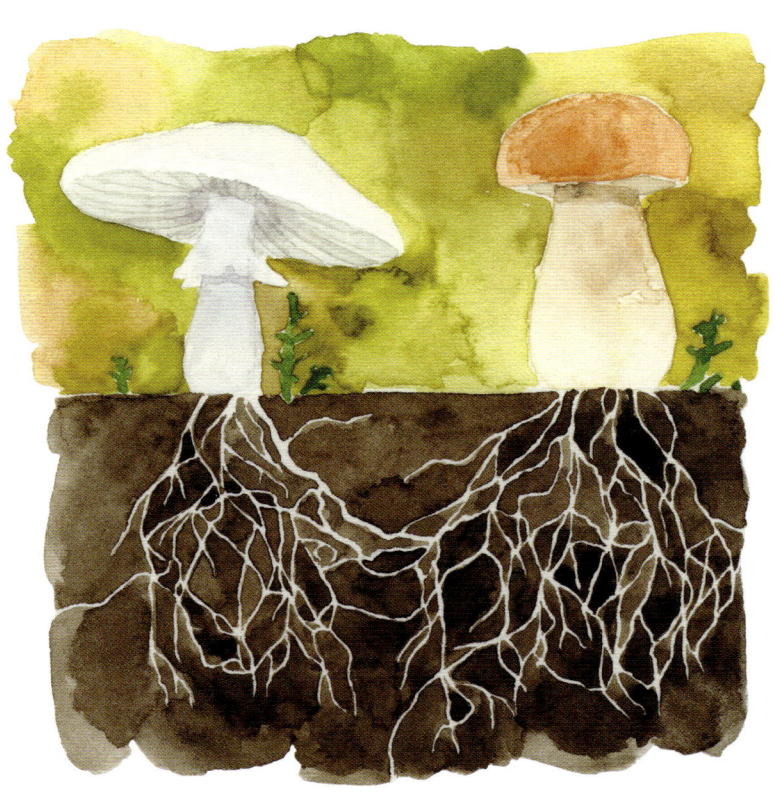

I IS FOR INTERGENERATIONAL

The next time you find yourself on a wooded trail, look for an old log that has been on the ground for a while. The more rot the better. Underneath, you will likely find fuzzy, white, cobweb-like threads that are called hyphae. They are the tip of a vast fungal network called mycelium that stretches much farther than you can see, binding the soil beneath your feet, weaving into tree roots at a cellular level, channeling nutrients, and redistributing resources throughout the entire ecosystem.

In recent decades, there has been an explosion of interest in these proliferating fungal networks, including mushrooms, which are the "fruit" of these organisms. Mycelia have been described as "the grand recyclers of our planet" because they disassemble larger molecules into simpler forms, creating ever thickening layers of soil, unlocking nutrients, and sharing them in ways that can regenerate depleted environments. Some researchers believe that mycelium is a key to our evolutionary survival.[1]

These densely interconnected networks have also evoked comparisons to the internet and have been nicknamed the "wood wide web." In this analogy, mycelium functions akin to fiber optic cables by providing the infrastructure for a vast subterranean communication system. Apart from allowing plants and trees to share resources—sugar, nitrogen, and phosphorus—this network also allows them to communicate in the manner of a social network. While we have known for some time that trees "talk" to each other across significant distances using airborne hormones, we are just beginning to understand what occurs beneath our feet.

I prefer Suzanne Simard's description of this network. Bypassing the technological metaphors, the forest scientist has shown how these fungal networks are patterned in ways that resemble the human brain (or perhaps more accurately, the human brain resembles these much more ancient networks). In the forest, trees actively perceive, communicate, and respond to one another by emitting chemical signals: *"Chemicals identical to our own neurotransmitters. Signals created by ions cascading across fungal networks."*[2]

Simard has shown that there is a generational structure to this underground network. Her research shows that older trees can discern which seedlings are their own kin, and they actively nurture them using the fungal network, sending food, water, and information as needed. When these "mother trees" die, they pass on their wisdom to their kin, sharing a lifetime of acquired knowledge about how to survive in an ever-changing environment.

This relatively new body of research on mycelium—a mass noun that puts pressure on the very idea of individuality—raises questions about where species begin and end, how all living things are radically interconnected, what counts as knowledge and communication, and how information is gathered, stored, and shared.

Long before this recent scientific furor, Sigmund Freud also turned to mycelium to describe dream life. In one of the most famous passages in *The Interpretation of Dreams*, Freud compares mycelium to the tangled mass of unconscious thoughts out of which a dream emerges (Freud regularly took his family to the mountains outside Vienna for holidays where they hiked, picnicked, and hunted for mushrooms):

> The dream-thoughts to which we are led by interpretation, cannot, from the nature of things, have any definite endings; they are bound to branch out in every direction into the intricate network of our world of thought. It is at some point where this meshwork is particularly close that the dream-wish grows up, like a mushroom out of its mycelium.[3]

I IS FOR INTERGENERATIONAL

This passage is usually understood to refer to the limitations of dream interpretation. The latent content of any given dream—what Freud calls the "dream-thoughts"—is so infinitely complex and leads in so many directions that aspects inevitably elude us. Freud calls this the "navel" of the dream. Even in the most obvious of dreams, he admits, contrary to his central thesis, there is a place that remains shrouded, a "spot where it reaches down into the unknown." The mycelium/mushroom model works effectively as a way to convey the relationship between the singularity of a dream and the vast network of ideas from which it grows—a network that has no definite endings and that reaches down into the unknown. The metaphor also works to highlight the generational quality of the intricate "world of thought" that dream life connects us to. The navel is, of course, a trace of a physical connection to our mothers through the umbilical cord.

When Freud's model of dream life is brought together with contemporary descriptions of mycelium, we see something that begins to resemble the idea of a collective unconscious, a vast web of communication that does not just connect individual human beings to each other (as Carl Jung imagined) but is something akin to the way Indigenous peoples describe our radical connectedness to the greater world, an understanding that "the life of one is dependent on the life of all."[4]

When my friend and colleague Lewis Williams formally introduces herself, she usually says, first in the Māori language and then in English: "My ancestors are of the people of Ngāi Te Rangi, Scotland, Wales and Germany. Ngāi Tūkairangi (Tauranga Moana) and Nan Ageantaich (Isle of Arran) are my clans. I grew up in Auckland and eventually returned to the Tauranga Moana, the homelands of my Ngāi Te Rangi ancestors. I am of that land. That is the land I was birthed to."[5]

Williams's area of research is human ecology—the study and practice of relationships between the natural and social environment. What she calls "radical human ecology" infuses Western definitions of the discipline with Indigenous methods that regard humanity as "an implicit part of biodiversity, embedded in a vast web of mutual and symbiotic interrelationships."[6] What drives her work is an effort to deepen our collective sense of relationality. Rather than focusing on whether the environment can absorb and adapt to human activity, Williams asks how we might we deepen our understanding of humanity's relationship with the living world.

This is why, in part, Williams introduces herself by describing her ancestors and the land from which she comes. Her sense of place in the world is derived from her connection to these ancestors—including Mauao, the sacred mountain of the Tauranga Moana tribe. In her case, this sense of connection was hard won. Growing up in Auckland, New Zealand, in the 1970s, she did not understand herself to be Indigenous. In fact, she once resigned from a job with the Department of Social Welfare so a Māori applicant could fill the role. At the time, Lewis was alienated from the Māori part of herself. As she put it, "I was long forgotten to my people, but worst of all, I was long forgotten to myself—to that part of myself."[7]

Lewis's ancestral inheritance came to her in fragments, in vague feelings, in snatches of conversation—and in dreams. In January 2000, while she was working on her PhD dissertation, she had a significant dream that she has named "Looking Back." It featured Jane Faulkner, one of her Māori ancestors whom she had just learned about:

> I am walking onto the *Marae* [a sacred community space] in search of the casket of Jane Faulkner, daughter of Ruawāhine Puhi, high class woman of the Ngāi Te Rangi tribe, and John-lees Faulkner, *Pākehā* [European] trader. I expect to see a Māori-looking woman in *Pākehā* clothing, because to me that's who Jane was—bilingual, schooled in both Māori and European ways. For me, though, her heart was Māori.
>
> I enter from the back. There is a group of *rangatahi* (youth) standing around. I walk by and look to them expectantly; they do not see me. I can see no coffin. I walk into the

wharekai (dining house) where there are some *wāhine* (women). Again they do not see me, do not greet me. I am invisible. I wander outside, feeling bleak. I look about. I had expected to see Jane lain out in her coffin in all her finery. I see no one, I see nothing . . . I am nothing.

I'm now on the wildest part of the *Marae*, the grass all long and overgrown. And then I see it. A coffin, lying in the long grass, in a state of disrepair, completely closed, one lid folded over the other, dusty, cobwebbed—long forgotten. I am long forgotten . . . to my *iwi* [people] and myself. I wake. I feel a deep despair.[8]

Williams awoke from this dream deeply disturbed. But as much as it left her with a sense of despair, it also compelled her to begin descending, climbing down what she calls an "*inner thread*, the thread of my Ngāi Te Rangi *tanga*." The dream functioned akin to the mycelium's hyphae—a thread that led her to a larger, intricately interconnected network of kin.

For many Indigenous knowledge keepers, dreams have long been understood to be portals for accessing the metaphysical dimension and a vital means for communicating with both the natural and spiritual worlds. Williams's dream of Jane Faulkner led her to begin reconstituting and deepening her sense of relationality through ancestral research, speaking with Ngāi Te Rangi elders, and eventually returning to Mauano, the esteemed mountain that stands guard at the entrance of Tauranga harbor. Through this work, Lewis discovered that in 1864, during Jane Faulkner's lifetime, her tribe's ancestral lands—including the sacred mountain—were confiscated by the colonial government of New Zealand. In the wake of this spatial and spiritual exile, Williams's great-grandfather moved to Auckland, and not until 2003 did Lewis and her mother reconnect with their ancestral lands and Ngai Te Rangi relatives.

It was a dream that called Lewis back, leading her to restore her connection with the land and her people—a return to the soil from which she came. Dreams, like mycelium, have the power to regenerate lifeworlds and even heal the wounds of history.

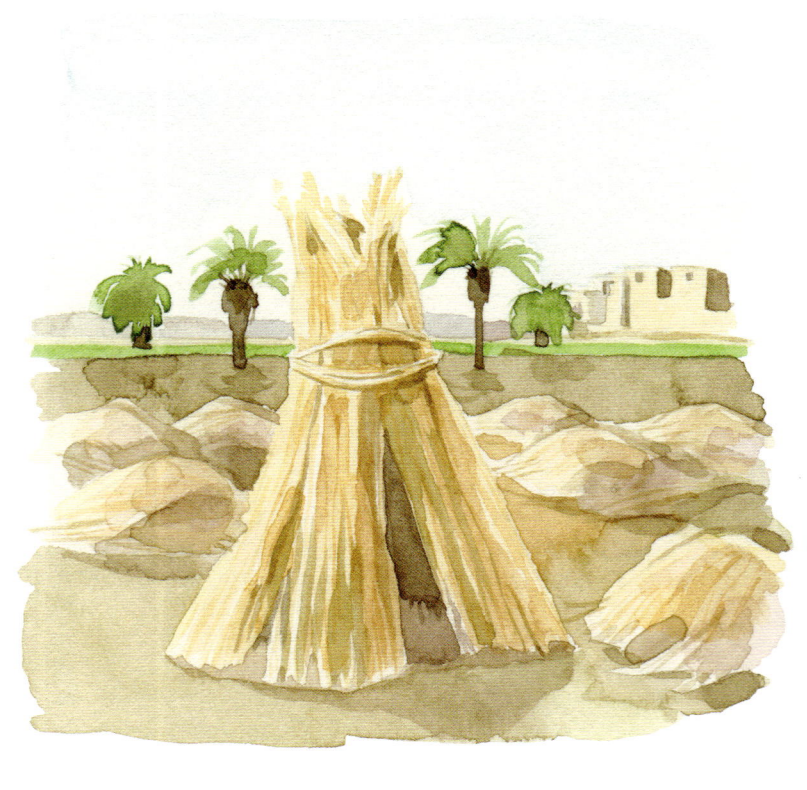

J IS FOR JEALOUSY

Dreams have always taken center stage in spiritual life. The authors of the Upanishads, the Indian spiritual doctrines that form the oldest scriptures of Hinduism, prized the inward-knowing dream state as superior to our waking view of the world. Dreams were crucial to the Buddha's enlightenment and to the Prophet Muhammad's (peace be upon him) revelations. In fact, attending these visions is a central tenet of all the Abrahamic religions.

Although I was never baptized, I grew up in a place where I heard Old Testament stories from an early age. My parents enrolled me in a nursery school that was connected to a local United Church of Canada, and before nap time, the staff read aloud stories from an illustrated children's Bible. I loved the story of Noah gathering animals into his big boat, and I can still recall my terror when I first heard about the binding of Isaac on Mount Moriah. But my favorite story was about Joseph.

Depending on your upbringing, you may know him as Yosef, Yusef, or even José. In the story I was told, Joseph was his father's favorite child, inspiring the envy of his many siblings. Jacob had twelve sons and one daughter born to several different mothers, but he loved Joseph more than all the rest because the boy was "the son of his old age," and he gave him a special, multicolored robe. When his brothers saw this, their envy of Joseph grew into hatred, and they "could not speak peaceably to him."[1]

When he was seventeen, Joseph had a dream in which he was with his brothers gathering wheat sheaves in the field. One of Joseph's sheaves suddenly stood upright, and his brother's sheaves came around and bowed down to it. When Joseph told his brothers about the vision, they asked, "Are you indeed to reign over us?" and hated him even more.

One day, Jacob sent Joseph to check on his brothers, who had brought the family's flock to Shechem. The brothers saw Joseph approaching from afar and plotted against him: "Here comes this dreamer. Come now, let us kill him and throw him into one of the pits, and we shall say that a wild beast has devoured him, and we shall see what will become of his dreams." But one of the brothers, Reuben, persuaded the others not to shed blood. They settled on a plan to sell him as a slave to a passing caravan that was on its way to Egypt. Once the transaction was complete, the brothers dipped Joseph's famous robe into goat blood and showed it to their father as proof that his son had been torn to pieces by a beast. Jacob grieved for many days and refused to be comforted.

After the caravan arrived in Egypt, Joseph was sold again, this time to Potiphar, the captain of Pharaoh's guard, but God looked upon Joseph with favor, and he prospered and eventually was appointed head of Potiphar's house. Joseph grew into a handsome man and Potiphar's wife became enthralled. One day, she tried to seduce him, and when he refused, the woman called the guards, claiming Joseph had violated her. Potiphar became enraged when he heard his wife's account and had Joseph sent to prison. But even in prison, Joseph had God's favor, and he prospered.

It was during his time in prison that Joseph developed his special understanding of dreams. When the royal cupbearer was also imprisoned for displeasing Pharaoh, Joseph offered an interpretation of one of his dreams, correctly predicting that he would be released and restored to his post in three days' time. Two years later, when Pharaoh himself became plagued by disturbing dreams, the cupbearer remembered the man he met in prison, and Joseph was summoned. Before revealing his dreams, Pharaoh demanded to know the source of Joseph's power, and he replied, "It is not I; God will give Pharaoh a favorable answer."[2] As was commonplace in the ancient world, Joseph understood dreams to be divine revelations, but he daringly proposed that the *one* God, the god of the Hebrews, would reveal the meaning of Pharaoh's dream.

Curiously persuaded by this response, Pharaoh shares his dreams in which he saw seven fat cows eaten by seven lean ones and seven good ears of grain swallowed by seven blighted ones. Joseph responded, "Pharaoh's dreams are one and the same. God has revealed to Pharaoh what he is about to do." The visions offer a glimpse of the future: seven years of prosperity will be followed by seven years of famine. Joseph counseled Pharaoh to prepare the country for a prolonged famine. Recognizing Joseph's percipience, Pharaoh declared, "Since God has shown you all this, there is no one as discerning and wise as you," and he placed his signet ring on Joseph's finger, making him the vizier of Egypt, second in command only to Pharaoh himself.[3]

When the predicted famine came to pass, many people in the region went hungry, including Joseph's family. The patriarch, Jacob, decided to send his sons to Egypt to try to buy food, since it was the only place that still had grain to sell. And so, twenty-two years after selling him into slavery, Joseph's brothers find themselves facing their younger brother, although this time, they do not recognize him. Once again in this ancient story, wisdom is defined as the power of discernment: Joseph can recognize his brothers, while they seem unable to see him, unable to recognize what is given to be seen.

After a series of tests to see if the brothers regret their betrayal, Joseph eventually reveals his identity to his siblings and forgives them. And since five more years of famine were yet to come, Joseph sends a caravan to the family to carry them to Egypt. When father and son finally lay eyes on one another, Joseph buried his face in his father's neck, and wept for a long time. Holding his son after so long, Jacob sighed: "I can die now, having seen for myself that you are still alive."[4]

This ancient story is widely understood to be one of the most powerful instances of dream divination—and there is much to be said about the hermeneutic method that Joseph employs—but to a child's ears, the story is about the terrible force of jealousy, the grace of forgiveness, and the radical possibility of reparation. As someone who grew up with two brothers, I intuitively understood the passions that drive the plot.

Along these lines, one of the more recent additions to clinical theory is an understanding of the social impact of sibling relationships. You are probably familiar with Freud's Oedipus complex, which focuses on the importance of the vertical axis (the relationship between children and parents) for psychosocial development. Much of the psychoanalytic literature is preoccupied with the force of this parental relationship. New research suggests that the horizontal axis (what happens between siblings) also has a powerful and long-term impact on our sense of self, our capacity to relate to others, and the world around us.

The British psychoanalyst Juliet Mitchell has proposed that the notorious tantrums that typically occur at age two—often called the "terrible twos"—are a moment of primary trauma.[5] Whether or not another child arrives in the family, the toddler becomes aware of the *idea* that another baby could stand in its place. At this crucial moment, our primary narcissism is threatened, and we are forced to become social creatures. For Mitchell, the fundamental task of becoming a member of the human society initially occurs through the interactions of siblings. While much of our social theory focuses on vertical interactions—lines of ascent and descent—Mitchell argues that looking laterally changes our view of the social contract. In this sense, our passage through sibling trauma is foundational to our ability to respond to and care for others.

This is where Joseph's story becomes exemplary. He is a survivor of his brothers' murderous rage. And his survival is owed, in no small part, to his capacity to attend to dream life. One of the lessons carried in this ancient story is that our ethics of care, and indeed, the strength and resilience of the social bond, rests on our ability to discern this other form of knowledge.

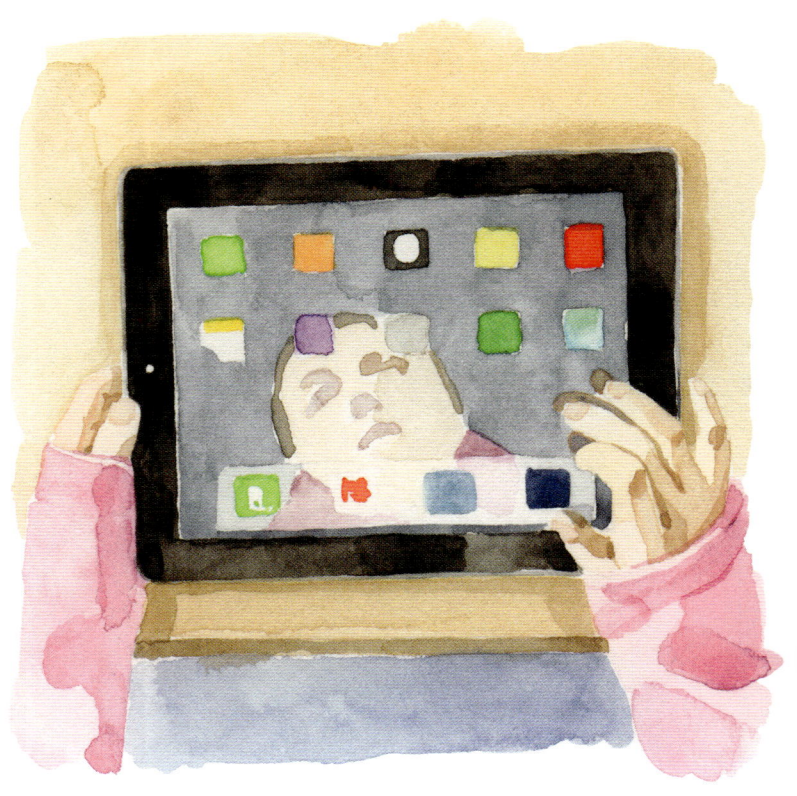

K IS FOR KIDS

When the COVID-19 pandemic began in March 2020, Iris was nine years old and living in Hackney, a culturally mixed neighborhood in East London.[1] Like many children her age, Iris was required to stay home from school when the British government implemented lockdown measures in March 2020. Teachers across the country hastily transformed their classrooms into online environments, often without training and, in many cases, without proper tools to connect with their students.

As many parents quickly realized, this mass experiment in remote learning exacerbated existing tensions in the school system. Several postpandemic studies have confirmed that the sudden shift online resulted in fewer children learning at grade level; increased inequity, anxiety, and loneliness; and more teacher burnout. The longer students remained away from in-person learning, the worse these effects became. Lower-income children and students of color in urban areas suffered the most acutely.[2] Already deprived of contact with their teachers, friends, and extended families, children were further benumbed by spending countless hours staring at a screen.

Prior to the pandemic, Iris was a prolific dreamer. Her mother had taught her daughter how to wake herself up in the middle of a frightening dream—a tool that proved useful during lockdown, when, like many people, Iris dreamed more vividly than she ever had before. Iris's mother had been taught this skill by her own mother. This ability to lucid dream—to be aware of the dream state and to have a limited ability to control the plot—seemed to pass only to female members of the family.

It is thought that humans begin dreaming in infancy, although we can know only after children develop enough linguistic capacity to describe them. We do know that children dream more frequently and with greater intensity than adults. Nightmares are common for children between the ages of three and nine. One study found that as many as 50 percent of children report frequent nightmares.[3]

The fact that children are especially prolific dreamers has led psychologists to seek developmental explanations. The Swiss psychologist Jean Piaget, for instance, proposed that dreaming serves the child's growing capacity for symbolic thought. In this respect, dreams are understood as akin to play. Both activities help children develop an understanding of the world they inhabit. While acknowledging this connection between dreams and play, Piaget also noted a distinction: dreams are not consciously made up in the same way as play. Indeed, dreams often feel all-too real, while children typically understand play to be make-believe.

Piaget proposed that the dream, like play, serves as a device that allows the child "to assimilate the whole of reality, *i.e.* to integrate it in order to relive it."[4] Put more plainly, dreams help us make sense of new experiences. We relive what we have experienced in our dreams as a way to "assimilate" the experience into our existing frameworks of understanding, or what Piaget refers to as "schemata." Dreams and play are a means for assimilating new information into our existing sense of the world.

But dreaming not only helps assimilate information into existing cognitive frameworks. These visions can also create entirely new schemata, generating a brand-new optic that transforms our understanding of the world. Piaget called this latter process "accommodation." So a dream can help us make sense of new experiences based on what we already know, but and it can also serve to create entirely new frameworks for understanding, enlarging our grasp of reality. This is another way saying that dreaming is world-making.

Iris's pandemic dreams provide a compelling example for Piaget's theory. During the first lockdown, Iris had a dream about her school that was situated entirely inside a virtual world.

It was a vaguely frightening dream for the nine-year-old: "I was a human in the virtual world," she reported. "I can feel myself tapping the keyboard on the iPad, but I can't take myself away from it. I can't turn my head or look around to see what's behind me. There's nothing. There's just a screen."

I shivered when I first heard Iris describe this dream. It was uncannily familiar, a precise description of what life felt like early in the pandemic, when everything moved to screens. At the end of long days filled with video meetings, I, too, felt trapped by my computer, unable to look away for fear of seeming disengaged.

During the second lockdown, Iris had a similar dream, but this time her class was transported into the world of *Minecraft*, a popular computer game (one of Iris's favorites) in which players discover and extract raw materials, craft tools, and build structures. In this second dream, Iris's school was set entirely within this characteristically pixelated world, and she was no longer fearful: "We were just doing normal *Minecraft* stuff," and some of her classmates even wore *Minecraft* "skins."

Both dreams are remarkable testimonies of a child's experience of the pandemic, but together they offer compelling evidence of the psychological labor involved in adjusting to the emergency measures. The first dream registers Iris's discomfort at transitioning to online learning—being frozen in a two-dimensional world where she was unable to turn her head or move away from the screen. In the second dream, her experience is more "assimilated," in Piaget's sense. School has morphed into a familiar virtual universe. Iris has found a way to make sense of her new experience, in part by relying on an existing schema—on something she already knows, *Minecraft*.

Children's experiences can be illuminating to adults because children spend a great deal of time actively constructing their understanding of the world. As they encounter new information, they must work to revise their existing schemata or invent entirely new schemata to make sense of new experiences. When my nephew saw a horse for the first time, he shouted, "Big doggy!"

My brother gently corrected him, "No, *horse*." My nephew's face was a wonder to behold as he processed this information, developing an entirely new mental category for this strange animal.

Iris taught me something about the pandemic, too. After the British government issued a third lockdown mandate, she had dream in which she and her mother had to have a surgery so she could return to her womb: "I was me, but I was just tiny" Iris reported. "And I had to go back inside. It got repeated many times. I kept getting put back in."

Iris's mother was intrigued by this dream, which she was hearing for the first time during our interview: "You had to go back inside mummy? How did you come out again?" Iris responded matter-of-factly: "They pulled my head." Iris's mother repeated her daughter's statement. "They pulled your head." Iris affirmed, "Yes, and all of a sudden it was really bright. It felt normal. A lot of people had to have it, and it was my turn, like the flu vaccine."

Iris's description stunned everyone, including our research team. After a beat, the nine-year-old dramatically enacted the last scene of her dream, contorting her body: "At the end of the dream, I came out in a loop de loop!" Iris's mother burst into peals of laughter at this strange image of her daughter somersaulting out of her womb. Iris did not know what this dream was about exactly, but she felt that it had to do with lockdown. As she put it, "because you have to go back into it." She felt this dream was her way of processing the repeated experience going "back into" lockdown.

Listening closely to her daughter's dream, Iris's mother turned to her daughter and offered her own intuitive account of what she had heard: "It is strange because I think that in our home, under lockdown, we do feel completely safe." And then, looking down at Iris, she repeated, "You feel really safe here in this house with us."

Listening to mother and daughter puzzle out the significance of Iris's dream brought home the radical nature of this communication, the importance of having another who is attuned to your lifeworld. In both profound and everyday ways, Iris's mother gave her mind over to her daughter in effort to help bring this dream—and by extension, her daughter's experience—into a shared world of meaning. The pediatrician Donald Winnicott named this deceptively simply act "holding," and he proposed that the "foundations of health are laid down by the ordinary mother in her ordinary loving care."[5] Winnicott noted that anybody (not only mothers) could perform this emotional function, and he extended its significance to school and other arenas of social life. It is both an ordinary and radical fact that we depend on others to sustain our sense of vitality. It takes (at least) two to dream.

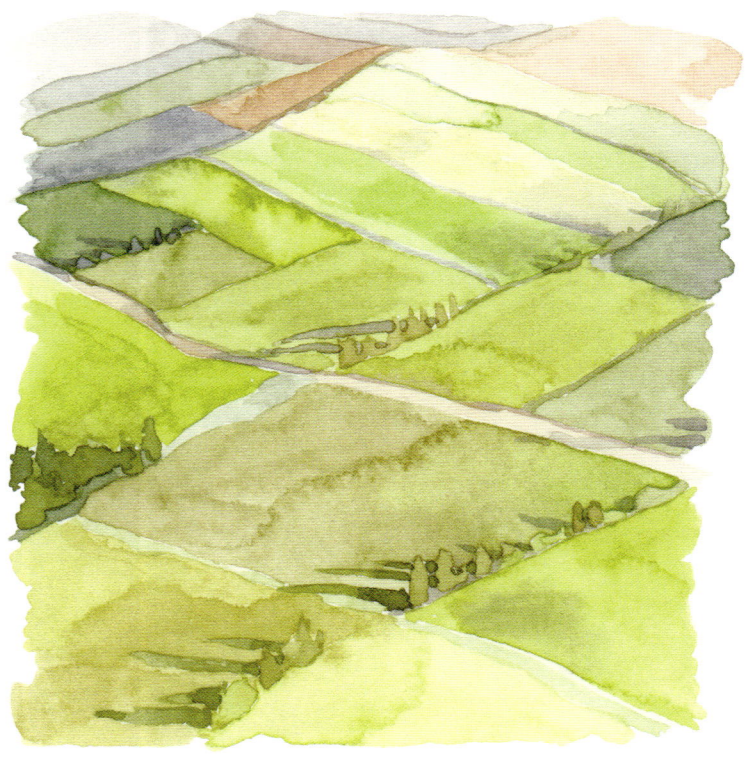

L IS FOR LIBERATION

The earliest known portrait of Harriet Tubman was made by the photographer Benjamin F. Powelson in 1868 or 1869. The portrait became a *carte de visite*—a collectible photographic calling card that was popular during the nineteenth century. This image was rediscovered in 2017 when a photographic album belonging to a white Quaker teacher named Emily Howland, who was Tubman's friend and neighbor, turned up at an auction. In the photograph, Tubman is seated sideways with one arm draped across the back of a wooden chair and the other resting on her checkered skirt, which flows voluminously to the floor. At the bottom of the image someone has written "Harriet Tubman" in pencil.

Tubman was in her mid-forties by the time this photograph was taken. Twenty years had passed since her escape from enslavement on the plantation in Maryland where she was born, and her days as one of the most successful conductors on the Underground Railroad were behind her. But before the Emancipation Proclamation of 1863, Tubman had returned to the Eastern Shore of Maryland at least thirteen times to liberate women, children, and men from the condition of slavery. She personally brought seventy people to freedom (as she put it, "never losing a passenger") and gave instructions to many more who sought their own liberation. During the Civil War, she led a band of scouts and became the first woman to lead an armed assault, liberating another 750 people from plantations along the Combahee River. Although she never held an official rank in the Union Army, she earned her nickname: "General Tubman."

The fact that no earlier photographs of Tubman exist (or have been found) is likely due to the nature of her work. She needed to

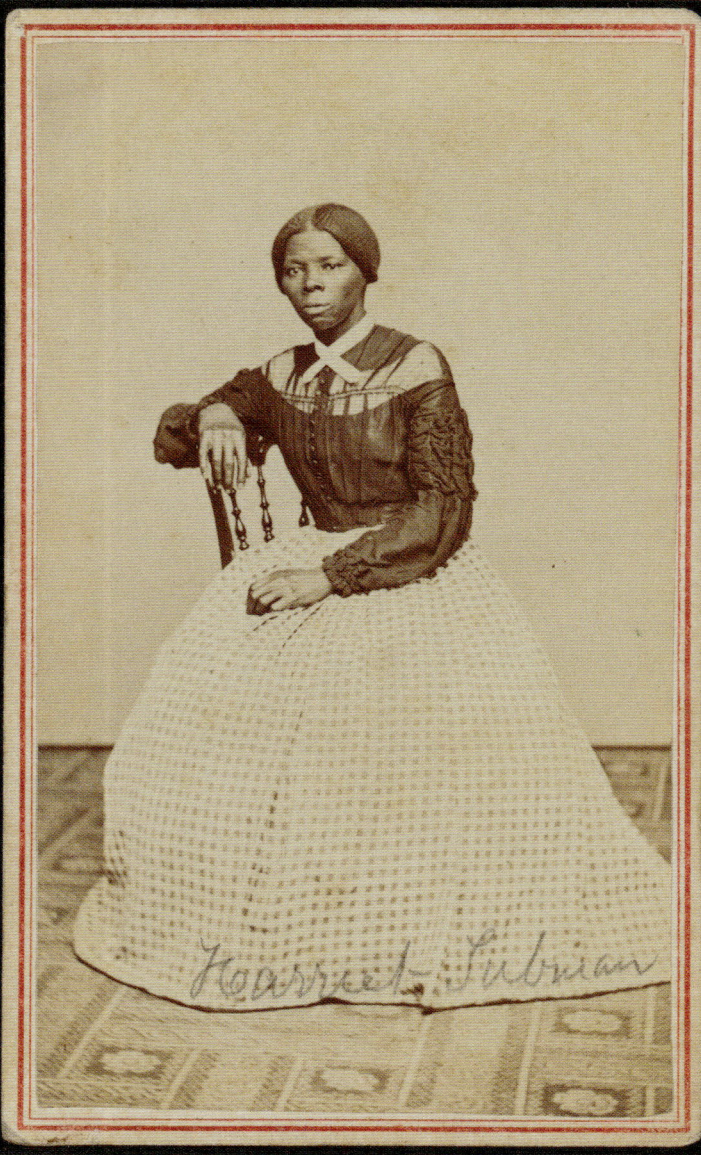

Harriet Tubman

Harriet Tubman. Photo courtesy of the collection of the
National Museum of African American History and
Culture shared with the Library of Congress.

following pages
Harriet Tubman's *carte de visite* in Emily Howland's album.
Photo courtesy of the collection of the National Museum
of African American History and Culture shared with the
Library of Congress.

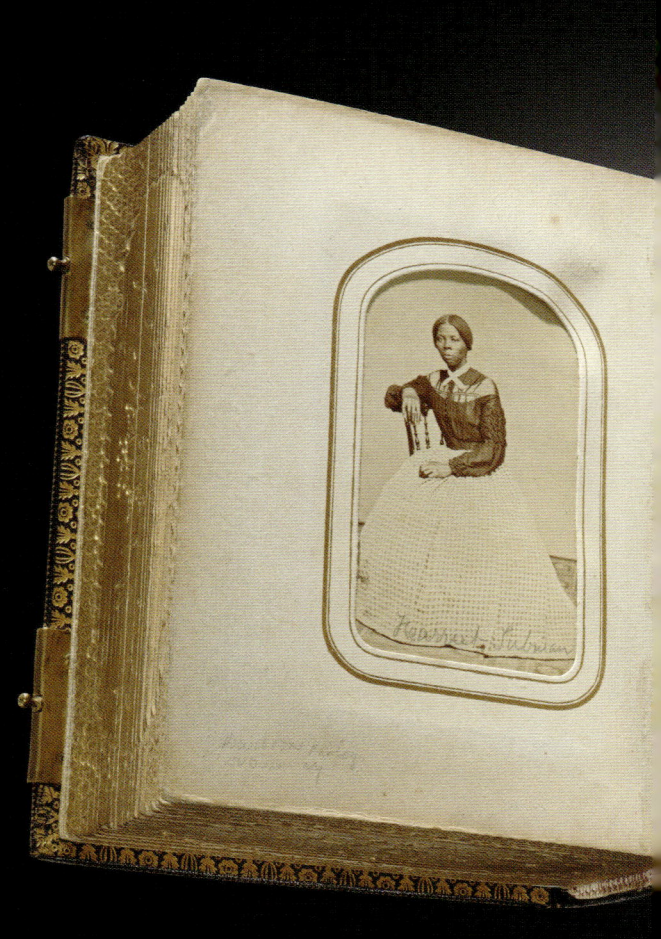

remain incognito. Before the abolition of slavery, slaveholders and slave catchers used photographic portraits to police subjects that were deemed to be white property, a legacy that persists whenever the medium is marshaled as a technology of racial surveillance. This same period is also replete with examples of the ways photography can be used to testify to freedom. By the time Tubman's portrait was made, her contemporary, Frederick Douglass, had posed for more than fifty different portraits and lectured on the virtues of the medium.[1] Tubman's *carte de visite* is a testament to both uses: it warns of the dangers of photographic capture *and* serves as statement of self-possession.[2]

Tubman could not read or write, so the story of her life survives through a series of mediated representations—including photographs. Although she certainly had a hand in crafting some of these representations, we do not have a direct account of her voice (unlike Douglass, whose legacy is defined by the words he put down on paper). A great deal of what we know of Tubman's life has been shaped by two biographies written by a white woman, Sarah Hopkins Bradford. The first book, *Scenes in the Life of Harriet Tubman*, was published in 1869, around the time that this photograph was taken (indeed, the photograph may have been taken for the occasion of the publication of the biography). In 1886, an expanded edition of this book, retitled *Harriet, the Moses of Her People*, was published.

It is important to underscore the mediated nature of Tubman's story and her image. While all her biographers note that Tubman credited her dreams and visions as the source of her singular ability to travel undetected through slave territory—her dreams served, quite literally, as a medium of liberation—we do not have a direct account of Tubman's interior life. Our understanding of this remarkable woman and the visions that guided her is inescapably mediated by a white imagination.

Imagination and, by extension, dream life, is not free from racism. As the poet Claudia Rankine and Beth Loffreda make clear, race enters writing "as a structure of feeling, as something that structures feelings, that lays down tracks of affection and repulsion, rage and hurt, desire and ache."[3] The mind's eye is not color-blind. Nor are any of our ways of seeing. All too often, as Tina Campt notes, white writers render Black life "in ways that allow it to be engaged at a safe distance or viewed at arm's length through a lens of pity, sympathy, or concern."[4] On other occasions, the white imagination seeks to violently inhabit Black experience.

This is also true in Harriet Tubman's case. The author of the preeminent narrative of Tubman's life is a white woman, and the only copy of the aforementioned photograph was (and remains) bound in a white woman's album. These conditions surrounding the representation of Tubman's life put pressure on the definition of liberation: Who gets to be the author of their own story? Who has control over the circulation of their own image?

Keeping these tensions in mind, Tubman's story remains important because it provides evidence of the remarkable role that dream life played—and continues to play—in the Black liberation struggle. In the antebellum era, enslaved people developed innumerable practices for cultivating an imagination that were antagonistic to the conditions of slavery. Dreams became one of the more important tools for refusing a system of value that transformed people into units of currency.

During her clandestine journeys back to the slave states of the South, Tubman recognized places she had seen in dreams and encountered people she had foreseen in visions. She understood this protective capacity for foresight to be a spiritual gift from God—with whom she kept a direct correspondence. In *Scenes in the Life of Harriet Tubman*, Bradford reports that Tubman evaded danger by "her quick wit, or by 'warnings' from Heaven."[5] Before her escape from slavery, Tubman told Bradford that she used to "dream of flying over fields and towns, and rivers and mountains, looking down upon them 'like a bird.'" Tubman was also known to regularly fall into a kind of somnolency, during which her spirit left her body to visit other scenes and places, "not only in this world, but in the world of spirits."[6]

This expansive form of communication that Tubman describes—including the communion of souls and spiritual revelation—was born, in part, as a response to the realities of plantation slavery. Slaveholders actively sought to keep the enslaved illiterate. After the revolt led by Nat Turner in 1831, most slave states passed laws that forbade the teaching of enslaved people to read and write. Black communities nevertheless developed complex and subversive systems of communication, what Booker T. Washington once referred to as "the grape-vine telegraph." These systems included the oral exchange of information at secret meetings but also more radical methods, such as call and response singing, signaling with light, and reading stars, omens, signs, and dreams. These were technologies of worldmaking, crucial gestures that helped sustain a vision of freedom to come. As the historian Saidiya Hartman has phrased it, these gestures functioned to sustain and create life in ways that "made it possible to survive the unbearable while never acceding to it."[7]

There is a deep and sustained record of attunement to dream life in the Black liberation struggle. Harriet Tubman's first public testimony, for instance, appears in 1856 in a book called *A North-Side View of Slavery. The Refugee: Or the Narratives of Fugitive Slaves in Canada*. The book is a collection of testimonies drawn from enslaved people who found their way to freedom in Upper Canada (the present-day province of Ontario), where slavery had been abolished. Tubman's is among the shortest testimonies in the book. She was relatively unknown in 1856 and probably wished to remain so. She encountered the book's author, Benjamin Drew, in St. Catharines, which was one of the terminuses of the Underground Railroad. She makes no mention of her work transporting refugees, revealing only that "I have seen hundreds of escaped slaves, but I never saw one who was willing to go back and be a slave."[8]

During his visit to St. Catharines, Drew also took testimony from a man named Isaac Williams, who had been enslaved on a plantation in Virginia. (Williams may well have been one of Tubman's "parcels.") His story is filled with scenes of the kind of brutality that was endemic to plantation life, but it is also filled with countless examples of the ways enslaved people challenged, refused, defied, and resisted the conditions of their enslavement. Williams, like Tubman, relied on his dreams to guide him to freedom. "For I'm never deceived in a dream," he reports: "That's as good a sign in the south as ever was."[9] His testimony includes a description of a prophetic dream that helped him in his initial escape from Virginia. After being recaptured and imprisoned, Williams received more guidance from his nocturnal visions. In another dream, he saw himself prying his way out of his prison cell and heard a man saying: "As long as there's breath there's hope." The man's voice awoke Williams, and the dream coaxed him to pry at the window frame in his cell, which eventually yielded the path of his escape.

Dream life continues to serve as an important resource for Black liberation. These visions have persistently guided those who find themselves on the front lines of the long struggle for freedom. In the last chapter of Assata Shakur's autobiography, she gives another account of a prophetic dream. In 1973, Shakur, a member of the Black Liberation Party, was traveling with two friends when their car was stopped by state troopers on the New Jersey Turnpike for a faulty taillight. The encounter that followed left her critically wounded and resulted in the deaths of two others, including one state trooper that Shakur was accused of murdering. Her autobiography describes the violence that Black revolutionaries faced (and continue to face): the routine racial profiling, the structural racism, and the pattern of mass imprisonment that was developed and deployed under the guise of the Nixon administration's "war on drugs."[10]

After a 1977 conviction for the murder of the state trooper and other felonies related to the highway shootings, Shakur was initially kept in solitary confinement for twenty-one months, was subject to beatings and vaginal and anal "searches," and was held as the only woman in a men's prison for a time. According to her attorney, Lennox Hinds, Shakur's autobiography understated the awful prison conditions: "in the history of New Jersey, no woman pretrial detainee or prisoner has ever been treated as she was, continuously confined in a men's prison, under twenty-four-hour surveillance of her most intimate functions, without intellectual sustenance, adequate medical attention, and exercise, and without the company of other women for all the years she was in custody."[11]

In the last chapter of her book, Shakur describes receiving a visit from her grandmother, who came from North Carolina to the New Jersey prison to tell her about a dream. According to Shakur, her grandmother's uncanny senses served like radar, picking up and identifying things that the rest of the family did not see: "My grandmother's dreams have always come when they were needed and have always meant what we needed them to mean. She dreamed my mother would be a schoolteacher, my aunt would go to law school, and during hard times, she dreamed the good times were coming."[12] For Shakur and her family, dreams provided guidance, but they did not weave a future on their own: "Dreams and reality are opposites. Action synthesizes them."

And so Shakur's grandmother came to the New Jersey prison to share what she had foreseen. The dream was set in their old family house in Jamaica: "'I dreamed I was dressing you,' she said, 'putting your clothes on.'" At first Shakur felt dread, thinking the dream was foretelling of her death. But her grandmother quickly reassured her: "No, you're alright. You're alive. It's just as plain as the nose on your face. You're coming home. I know what I'm talking about. Don't ask me to explain it anymore, because I can't. I just know you're going to come home and that you're going to be all right."[13]

In 1979, not long after her grandmother's visit and with the help of members of the Black Liberation Army, Assata Shakur escaped from the Clinton Correctional Facility and eventually made her way to Cuba, where she was granted political asylum, and where—despite several extradition attempts—she continues to live today in freedom.

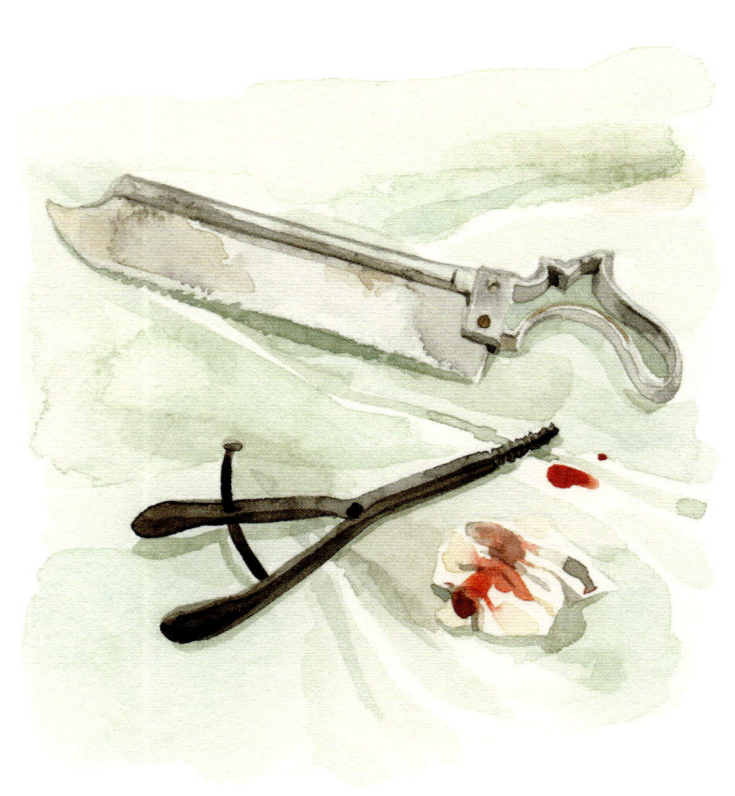

M IS FOR MONSTER

The first edition of *Frankenstein; or, The Modern Prometheus* was published in three volumes on January 1, 1818. In an eerie parallel of the titular character's central conflict, the author's name was conspicuously absent from that first edition. Not until several years later did Mary Wollstonecraft Godwin take responsibility for her "hideous progeny," although by that time she had become Mrs. Percy Bysshe Shelley.

The story of Victor Frankenstein and his lonely monster has preoccupied our collective imagination for more than two hundred years. It has been subject to countless interpretations and adaptations and continues to be reinvented because it resonates with many of our ongoing concerns—the perils of scientific discovery and biological engineering, artificial intelligence, economic disparity, ambition, racism, birth and abortion, loneliness, and perhaps most universally, the anguish of a life exiled from love.

In an 1831 edition, Mary Shelley provided an introduction designed to satisfy readers who were skeptical about how a young woman could produce so hideous a tale. In it she reveals the origins of her novel in a story that has become almost as famous as the book itself.

Mary recalls how she and her husband, Percy Bysshe Shelley, spent the summer of 1816 on Lake Geneva. She does not mention that her stepsister Claire accompanied them, that Percy was married to another woman, and that both the Godwin and Shelley families had all but renounced ties to the couple. Lord Byron and his doctor, William Polidori, were also staying on the lake, and on rainy days, members of the group entertained themselves by reading a book of German ghost stories to one another. After one of these sessions, Byron challenged everyone to try writing a frightening tale.

Mary describes struggling for days with "that blank incapability of invention which is the greatest misery of authorship, when dull Nothing replies to our anxious invocations." But one night, after listening to Byron and Shelley debate the science of galvanism late into the night, likely under the influence of copious amounts of alcohol and laudanum, she went to bed and promptly found herself in the middle of a waking dream:

> When I placed my head on my pillow, I did not sleep, nor could I be said to think.
>
> My imagination, unbidden, possessed and guided me, gifting the successive images that arose in my mind with a vividness far beyond the usual bounds of reverie. I saw— with shut eyes, but acute mental vision—I saw the pale student of unhallowed arts kneeling beside the thing he had put together. I saw the hideous phantasm of a man stretched out, and then, on the working of some powerful engine, show signs of life, and stir with an uneasy, half vital motion. Frightful must it be; for supremely frightful would be the effect of any human endeavour to mock the stupendous mechanism of the Creator of the world.[1]

This remarkable vision gave rise to one of the most enduring themes in literature—Victor Frankenstein's spectacular failure to take responsibility for his "creation."

As many critics have pointed out, behind this dream of the dead brought back to life lies another dream about an equally disastrous birth.[2] Sixteen months prior, on February 22, 1815, seventeen-year-old Mary Shelley gave birth to her first child. The baby girl was two months premature and, like Frankenstein's creature, bore no name. Following Victorian custom, Mary and Percy refrained from naming a child who was not expected to live. After a week of favorable signs, Mary began to hope that the baby might survive, but eleven days after the birth, she awoke to find her baby dead. The shock was compounded by the eerie parallel to Mary's own birth: eleven days after Mary was born, her own mother, Mary Wollstonecraft, had died.

On March 19, the bereaved mother wrote in her journal: "Dream that my little baby came to life again—that it had only been cold & that we rubbed it by the fire & it lived—I awake & find no baby—I think about the little thing all day—not in good spirits." A few days after that, another entry in her journal: "Dream again about my baby—[?—————————————]"[3]

The brackets and dashes indicate "unrecovered cancelled matter"; someone may have blotted out the entry or torn a page out of the journal. What is known for certain is that Mary Shelley dreamed that her dead baby came back to life. And then she dreamed of it again. And then sixteen months later, came the vision of Frankenstein infusing the spark of life into his creation.

Given this remarkable trajectory and the way that loss piled upon loss throughout Mary Shelley's life, it is possible to read *Frankenstein* as a prolonged meditation on the force of grief—not just the familiar sadness that comes with any meaningful loss but the acute kind of grief that can twist a soul into bitterness and despair. Mary Shelley was certainly no stranger to these feelings: grief is one of the most common descriptors used in Frankenstein's confessions. The interpretations of the story that fixate on the scientist's ambition and his godlike ability to animate life often miss the unrelenting anguish that drives this character.

At the beginning of Victor's confessions (which are embedded in the novel's epistolary framing), he describes an idyllic childhood and his passion for natural science. But at age seventeen—the same age Mary Shelley lost her baby—Victor's life is marred by tragedy. His beloved mother is struck down by scarlet fever, and although her death is described as a calm one, Victor cannot bear the loss:

I need not describe the feelings of those whose dearest ties are rent by that most irreparable evil, the void that presents itself to the soul, and the despair that is exhibited on the countenance. . . . When the lapse of time proves the reality of the evil, then the actual bitterness of grief commences.[4]

Frankenstein leaves for university under this cloud of "evil" and quickly becomes morbidly preoccupied with death, fervently analyzing "all the minutiae of causation" until one night, he discovers the secret that animates life.

When he finally manages to bring his monster to life, he is filled with horror and disgust. He abandons his newborn creation and rushes to his bedroom to seek the escape of sleep. But his rest is disturbed by "the wildest dreams": he dreams that as he embraces his beloved fiancée, Elizabeth, she turns into the corpse of his dead mother, complete with grave worms crawling in the folds of her shroud.

A strange demand comes with a great grief, Mary Shelley's book seems to suggest—a weird kind of responsibility to become equal to what has been lost. We must create something from our pain that feels adequate to our experience of the loss. But depending on the circumstances, this emotional demand can go horribly wrong. And so monsters are born.

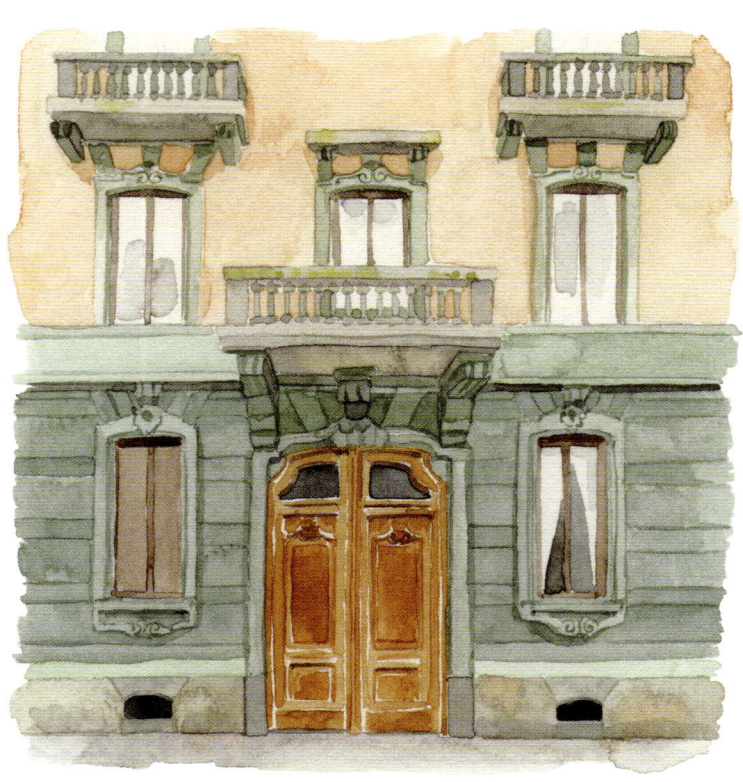

N IS FOR NIGHTMARE

What is a nightmare but an inexplicable experience of being violently awoken, drenched in fear and anguish? The plots of these dreams are often dramatically cut off so that the usual protective function of dream life is short-circuited. This combination of extreme emotion and narrative breakdown can drive a desperate need for contact. Awaking in a fright, we spontaneously seek out the protective embrace of someone with whom we can share the terrifying experience.

Nightmares are the closest that many of us will come to psychosis. What causes this class of dreams is an unresolved question. Contemporary neuroscientists are split about whether nightmares represent an intensified version of dreaming (in their terms, a key neurobiological process that enables emotional regulation and cognitive adaptation) or, conversely, whether they are evidence of the breakdown of this process.[1] Either way, the extreme distress that these dreams can create reveals how wounding it can be when our capacity to make meaning breaks down.

When people ask me about nightmares, the example that often comes to mind is from *Se questo è un uomo*, the 1947 memoir written by the Italian chemist and Auschwitz survivor Primo Levi.[2] (The memoir was originally translated into English as *If This Is Man* and later republished in the United States as *Survival in Auschwitz*.) Levi's memoir has been hailed as one of the most important testimonies of the twentieth century. In it, he relates several dreams that visited him while he was a prisoner in Auschwitz, but one stands out.

One night, after dreaming uneasily of the day's events in the concentration camp, Levi awakes and immediately falls back asleep, where he dreams that he is back home in Turin. He is in his family's apartment with his sister and several unidentifiable friends. Levi describes the feeling of being home among friendly people as an "intense pleasure, physical, inexpressible."[3] He has much to tell them about the camp—the trains, the single bunk he shared with another man, the gnawing hunger, the humiliating lice control, the kapo who beat him.

But as he relays his story in the dream, Levi realizes that his sister and his friends are not listening to him: "In fact, they are completely indifferent: they speak confusedly of other things among themselves, as if I was not there. My sister looks at me, gets up and goes away without a word." This sudden realization that his audience is indifferent brings "a desolating grief," a feeling of "pain in its pure state, not tempered by a sense of reality and by the intrusion of extraneous circumstances, a pain like that which makes children cry."[4]

The memoir goes on to describe how Levi realizes, moments after resurfacing from the nightmare, that this is not a haphazard vision but one that he has dreamed many times since arriving in Auschwitz. It is a recurring nightmare that hardly varies in terms of details or environment.

In fact, Levi realizes that he has already recounted the dream to his friend Alberto. And to his surprise, Alberto confides that he has also experienced a version of this dream—sharing the horrors of the camp to a completely indifferent audience. Many prisoners have had this dream, Levi admits, "perhaps everyone." But why? "Why is the pain of every day translated so constantly into our dreams, in the ever-repeated scene of the unlistened-to story?"[5]

The shared nature of this nightmare is part of what distinguishes it. Levi's testimony highlights our common and primal need for our voices to be heard and for our experiences to be received and confirmed by our community. Conversely, *not* being listened to—having friends and family respond with indifference

—undermines or even negates our experience, leaving behind a destabilizing sense of *un*reality. Without a receptive audience, it is difficult for Levi and his fellow prisoners to hold onto their existential bearings. The nightmare is evidence for the ways that we need one another to anchor us in the world, as if the moorings of our being are indivisibly tethered to the other's recognition.

Apart from the year he spent in Auschwitz and the immediate months after liberation, Primo Levi was firmly rooted in his world. He lived in the same apartment in Turin for his entire life, and his two children lived nearby. Until he retired, he worked at the same paint factory, first as a chemist and then as a manager. Levi's elderly mother lived with him and his wife until he died in 1987 after he fell in the stairwell of his apartment building. (The death was officially ruled a suicide, although he left no note and there were no witnesses.)

After the publication of his memoir, Levi was repeatedly asked for his thoughts about survival: what was the secret for surviving the horrors of Auschwitz? It is a cruel question, especially given the depth of guilt Levi expressed about having survived when so many did not. In one of the last interviews before his death, he was faced with the question once more: "As for survival, this is a question that I put to myself many times and that many have put to me. I insist there was no general rule, except entering the camp in good health and knowing German. Barring this, luck dominated. I have seen the survival of shrewd people and silly people, the brave and the cowardly, 'thinkers' and madmen."[6]

Levi acknowledged that he was attentive to the world and people around him, so much so that he could still call up an "unbelievably detailed image of them." This attentiveness was also a survival tactic: life in Auschwitz was radically unstable (especially toward the end of the war while Levi was imprisoned there), and the ability to distill a degree of coherence kept him alive. But this drive to make sense out of a senseless situation also carried over into the writing of his memoir:

I wrote *If This Is Man* struggling to explain to others, and to myself, the events I had been involved in, but with no definite literary intention. My model (or if you prefer, my style) was that of the "weekly report" commonly used in factories: it must be precise, concise, and written in a language comprehensible to everybody.[7]

To my ears, this suggests Levi's memoir can also be understood to be a response to his nightmare. The chemist felt compelled to find a way to convey the events he experienced in a manner that would secure his listener's attention. His survival depended on overcoming a terrifying indifference and on his ability to render the events he witnessed in a way that was comprehensible to everybody.

Levi opted for the clear and transparent language of the factory, and in a sense, this approach proved successful: he became a prominent voice after the war, recognized worldwide as one of the most important interpreters of the Shoah. His books continue to be widely read, and his testimony has been particularly influential to debates about the role of memory in shaping society. He wrote several more works of fiction and nonfiction, meditating not only on his time in the death camp and its anguished and insoluble legacy but also on more contemporary threats to human dignity.

But this public recognition failed to stop the nightmare of "the unlistened-to story" from returning. At the same time that his writings worked to secure the legacy of the Shoah in cultural memory, Levi was growing increasingly distressed about how this legacy was becoming usurped by Israel and its supporters. For all his care in describing his experience of the Nazis death camps with precision and economy, a distorted consciousness of the Shoah was emerging. A political faction that had gained power in Israel began exploiting the Holocaust as justification for its violent military aggression under the guise of national self-defense. The Nazi attack on human dignity that Levi described had become justification for the annihilation of Israel's enemies, including the systematic repression of the Palestinian people.

In 1982, Levi publicly stated his opposition to Israel's bombing of Beirut and its responsibility for the Lebanese Forces' massacres in the Sabra and Shatila neighborhoods, which killed thousands of Arab civilians.[8] He also felt that, as a Jew, he had a responsibility to publicly oppose the building of Israeli settlements in Israeli-occupied Palestinian territories.[9] In letters and interviews from the end of his life, the author tried to refute those who called upon the memory of the Shoah to legitimate lethal violence against civilian populations.

At a 1985 talk in New York, Levi was asked for his opinion on Middle East politics. When he started to say that "Israel was a mistake in historical terms," he was cut off by shouts from audience members that forced the moderator to halt the meeting. Heated attacks on the author followed in print, and Levi later admitted the response had extinguished his "will to live."[10]

Part of what makes nightmares so disturbing that they can bring the dreamer to thoughts of suicide is the way these visions dramatize what might be our fundamental existential threat—facing the "ever-repeated scene of the unlistened-to story."

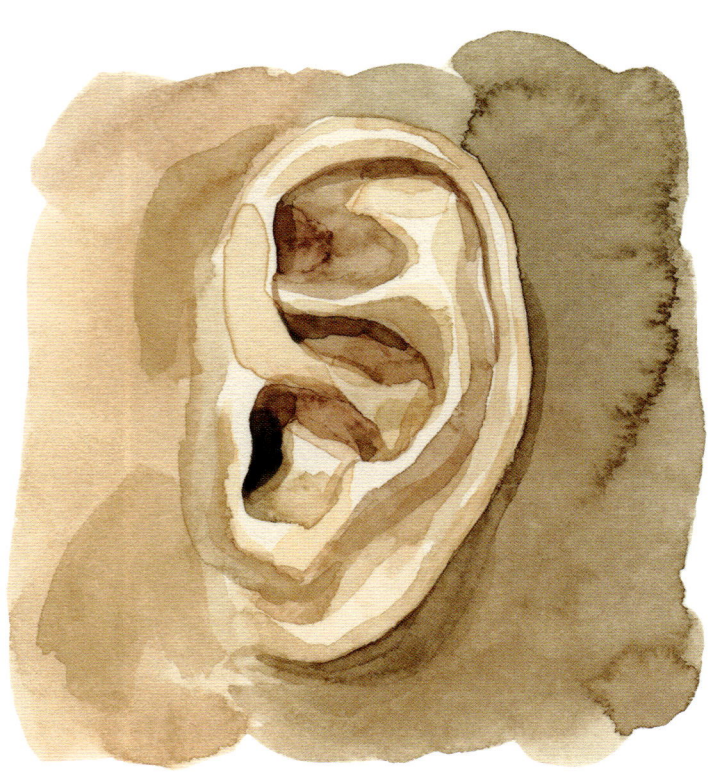

O IS FOR OTOSCOPE

One of the first people I interviewed for our study about how COVID was affecting the dream life of Londoners was Dr. Ishani Rao. Rao had been working almost nonstop since the pandemic began. When it started, she was on leave from her emergency room training but was called back to work on the COVID wards. That was when she started having "crazy intense dreams."[1]

Rao was not alone. In the spring of 2020, when stay-at-home directives were in wide effect, mainstream media outlets reported on a global increase in vivid and bizarre dreams, many of which concerned coronavirus and social distancing. Social media hashtags mentioned lockdown dreams and COVID nightmares. The two most common words that showed up in our interviews were "vivid" and "intense."

When I spoke to Rao by video call in February 2021, she was at home on her day off. Throughout our conversation, she radiated a sense of vibrancy. Here was a junior doctor who, despite—or perhaps because of—the unprecedented pressures of the past year, was eagerly on the side of life.

In July 2020, Rao had somehow managed to find time to publish a book called *National Health Stories: Tales from the Front Line*.[2] As the title suggests, the book gathers narratives and anecdotes from people working for the UK National Health Service. In one entry, a doctor laments the fact he can no longer drink his favorite beer because of its name (Corona). In another story, a nurse describes being called in to work one night on a new VIP ward that had just one patient who was mysteriously listed on the chart as "Quebec Zulu." (The nurse notes that this also happened to be the same night that Prime Minister Boris Johnson was taken to the hospital with severe COVID symptoms.)

Rao's contribution to the collection was a dream report. She was still laughing about the dream when shared it with me:

> I dreamt that I was on the ward and I had to look into a patient's eardrum using an otoscope—the device that you used to look into people's ears if they've got an infection or if you want to see the eardrum. I looked down the ear canal and I saw a healthy cervix as if I was doing a smear test. But in the patient's ear. In my dream, I said: "A smear test" and the ear kind of stood out. I told patient that the exam was normal, and I woke myself up laughing.

When I asked Rao what she thought about her dream, she laughed again and pointed out the pun on "ear" and "smear," which seemed to delight her. But after a beat, her mood grew more sober. She noted that the dream felt all too real: "I really thought that it was real life. I was walking down the corridor, I was checking my bag to make sure that I had all of the equipment that I needed, I was putting on the personal protective equipment." Rao was working on the COVID wards at the time and felt that the dream was an extension of what she had been doing every day for the past year. It was only when she looked in her patient's ear that she sensed something was not quite right.

I asked Rao what she thought about the image of the cervix. She laughed again and pointed out that at least it was a "healthy" cervix:

> I told my patient: "Okay, it's normal." But I didn't even feel relieved in my dream that it was normal. I just thought, "Okay, I've done my job. Now I'll just go onto the next." I think that's striking because speaking to a lot of my friends who've had anxiety about the last year, it's been difficult to gauge what's normal and what's not. What's a healthy level of anxiety to have? What is a normal level of nightmares or dreams to have? It's really difficult to tell what's normal in such a new situation. For me, to have dreams which are relatively nice and normal and healthy, that makes me really

happy when I wake up. But then again, there's also the other side where I wake up and I feel very anxious and stressed, and those dreams have become a lot more regular since COVID started.

In our conversations with Londoners, our research team encouraged the dreamers to provide their own thoughts about the meaning of their visions rather than offer interpretations of our own. The project was partly guided by Erik Erikson's description of the "intellectual partnership" between clinician and patient.[3] Contemporary clinicians emphasize the importance of symbolization—the way that speaking about a dream can allow unspoken material to be expressed. Dreams can push dreamers to symbolize the things they have trouble expressing otherwise, and our research team understood that our primary role was to facilitate and encourage this expression of the thoughts, feelings, and ideas that people struggle to voice to themselves and to each other.

But this "intellectual partnership" also involves a delicate kind of parallel play on the part of the listener. As our team listened to the participant's dream reports, we were attentive to the involuntary thoughts and images that passed through our own minds. Theodor Reik called this technique "listening with the third ear."[4] Here listeners play the role of sounding board, giving themselves over to receiving the unconscious elements of the communication, which can also register as reveries in a listener's mind. This is a radical approach to listening: here the thoughts, feelings, and images that come into the listener's mind are understood to be an extension of the dreamwork. The listener's mind becomes a receptive instrument in the larger process of symbolizing what is not yet conscious in the dreamer.[5]

When Rao described her dream of looking into her patient's ear with an otoscope, what came into my mind was Freud's dream of "Irma's injection." This is perhaps the most famous dream in the psychoanalytic cannon and I will not try to summarize exhaustive commentary surrounding it. (Erikson offers an excellent account in his celebrated essay, "The Dream Specimen of Psychoanalysis."[6]) I suspect Freud's dream came to mind because the main scene is strikingly similar to Rao's dream. In Freud's dream, he also conducts an examination of one of his patients, but rather than look into the ear, Freud peers into his patient's mouth. And in both dreams, the doctors see something that belongs to another area of the body. In Freud's dream, he looks into his patient's mouth and sees "remarkable curly structures which were evidently modelled on the turbinal bones of the nose." In Rao's dream, she looks into her patient's ear and sees a healthy cervix.

As my conversation with Rao continued, the echoes between her dream and Freud's deepened. After sharing her otoscope dream, Rao told me about a "horrible" situation at work that occurred weeks earlier but was still on her mind. As she put it: "a patient died who shouldn't have died." The patient was fifty-nine and came into the ER after a heart attack. Rao managed him "immaculately," as she put it, but after the initial treatment, he was transferred to another hospital, where he subsequently died. The situation prompted Rao to wonder about her own behavior: "If I had known that he was going to die, would I have just put a bit more of a human spin on it? Would I have at least said to him, 'How's your year been? Do you want a cup of tea?' Just something more human."

These questions persisted in Rao's mind. Her colleagues reassured her that she had done everything right: she managed the patient's heart attack and transferred him to the next hospital, which followed proper procedure. Her job demanded that she move on to the next patient, not to stop and ask if any patients wanted a cup of tea. But despite these reassurances, Rao turned the "horrible situation" over and over in her mind for weeks and even wrestled with it her dream life: "I can tell that the feelings [in the dream] are related to that. I think it's my body trying to tell me, 'You need to let it go. You've tried to do what was best for that patient.'"

A strikingly similar emotional situation lies behind Freud's famous "specimen dream." In his associations to the dream, Freud (who also was a junior doctor at the time), admitted the dream brought to mind a situation involving one of his colleagues, Dr. Wilhelm Fliess, who was a nose and throat specialist and to whom Freud had referred one of his own patients for further treatment. In his published account of the dream, Freud does not mention that Fliess conducted a disastrous operation on the patient in question that almost killed her. (Fliess left gauze in the patient's nose cavity after surgery, and two weeks later, when the patient was back in Freud's care, she suffered a massive hemorrhage.) Freud was not responsible for the medical misconduct, but in a private letter, he admits feeling haunted by the incident and plagued by doubt. Two months later, he dreamed his famous dream.[7]

Given the nature of the medical profession, it seems obvious that doctors would dream of medical examinations and treatments. And in times of crisis, it seems obvious that their dreams would document the emotional weight of what it means to be responsible for the lives of others. But the medical literature on physician burnout tends to focus more on the structural and cultural problems of medical practice and less on physicians' emotional lives. The literature that does look at the emotional lives of doctors reveals that one of the chief emotional challenges of practicing medicine is hidden guilt, particularly a feeling of guilt even when they have done nothing wrong.[8] Dreams manifest the emotional strains of the profession. But Rao's example shows that they can also help protect against these invisible wounds.

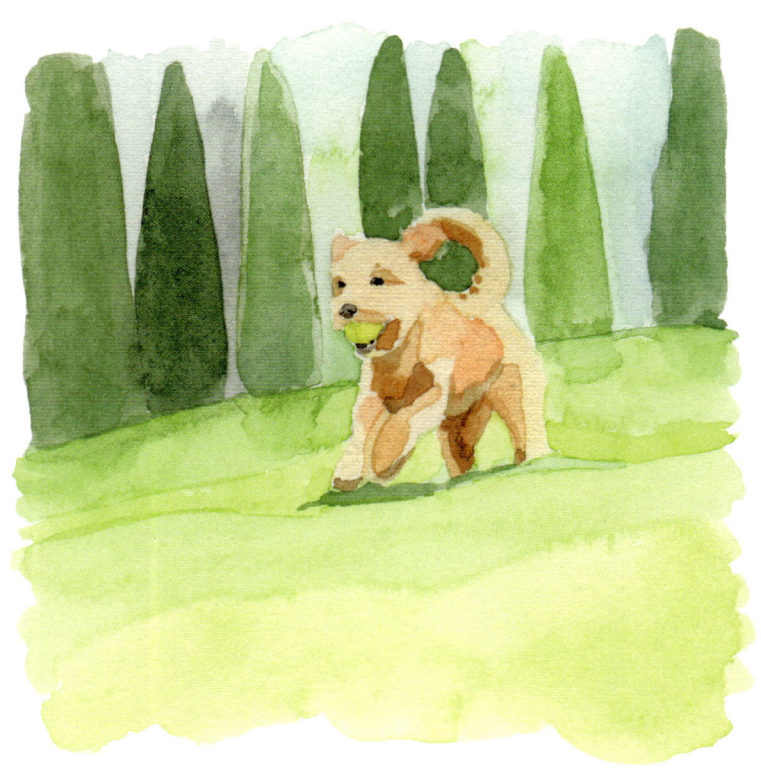

P IS FOR PRINCESS DIANA

A vibrant young woman introduces herself casually over Zoom: "Hi, I'm Kavita. I was born in London. Been living here pretty much all my life."[1] The vertical sliver of her screen is just wide enough to hold her face. Behind her is a vivid, flowered wallpaper, which makes her appear to be floating in a sea of pink and red blooms.

About a year into the pandemic, Kavita responded to our research team's public call for participation in a study about how COVID-19 was affecting the dream life of people living in the British capital. She described herself as a prolific dreamer. She often had multiple dreams a night but rarely recorded them: "Somehow, I tend to just remember them." She had developed her own unique method of "pondering" over her dreams, which began by asking herself, "Why am I having such a dream?" For Kavita, attending to her dreams was a spiritual practice: "I'm still learning, but from my current perspective and from the experiences I've had, I feel like dreams are a window to our soul." She laughed. "I know that sounds a bit dramatic, but I honestly feel that."

Kavita spoke to our study group in February 2021. She told us that her curiosity about dreams led her to join a "social dreaming" group that met online during the pandemic. Social dreaming is an experimental method for sharing dreams that was developed in the 1980s at the Tavistock Institute of Human Relations in London. Although the method borrows from some of the principles of group psychology, social dreaming is not a therapeutic practice and is not focused on group dynamics per se. People come together to discuss their dreams as a kind of cultural resource. Personal meaning is set aside in favor of using dreams as a way to think through shared social concerns.

Kavita shared some of the material that her group had been discussing: "A lot of war dreams have been coming up. Dreams about concentration camps and things from the past. A lot of dreams about survival. I had a dream where I was struggling to survive. I had to think on my feet, 'How am I going to survive this?'" Kavita understood these dreams to be in direct dialogue with the pandemic: "We're all just trying to survive this. We're talking about rationing, and we're back to long food cues. These are things from the past."

Kavita took her time deciding whether she trusted our research team. Eventually, it became clear that she wanted to share a particular dream. She was deliberate in her recounting of it, choosing which details to include and which to withhold:

I'm in a church. It's a really, really beautiful church. In front of me I'm seeing a few people coming into the church. It seems like a ceremony for someone's funeral. The body is right at the front of the church in a coffin. This gentleman is of black origin. I know in the dream that this person has been very well respected, and people are really devastated that he has gone, that he's passed away. People are coming in and sharing their respects. I'm hovering over and watching people coming in and out.

And then I step out of this church and enter this beautiful park. I'm aware that it's in London. It reminds me of Regent's Park. On my left, I see trees and people having picnics sitting outside. It's beautiful. The weather is amazing. And on my right, I see a gate. It's like a mini graveyard but not a graveyard—a place of remembrance. People are paying respect to those that have passed away. I'm watching, seeing who is there. I notice someone from my own religion, which is Hindu, and I see a god that I actually believe in. I pay my respects, and I think, "Wow, this is amazing." I've managed to get some blessings here.

I walk on. I'm strolling through this park. And then I see a small dog playing around. It's really cute. And then I see

Princess Diana sitting on a bench. She's playing with the dog. She can't see me. I'm just watching her, and she's so happy. She just seems so happy. And then I wake up.

Kavita could not remember which month she had this dream in, but it was during 2020, a year that was dominated by the pandemic and marked by racial violence, including the murder of George Floyd, which generated worldwide protests. Given the dream's proximity to these events, it was hard not to understand it as a dialogue with the news headlines.

But what kind of dialogue? Kavita's dream landscape does not exactly bear witness to a violent death. Rather, she attends a funeral, hovering above the scene as people pay their respects to the black man inside a beautiful church. The dream stages a series of mourning scenes for public figures—scenes of grieving, scenes of remembrance, scenes of commemoration. It is a dream about care, not spectacular violence. It stages and performs the rituals of mourning that help render lives *grievable*.

The American philosopher Judith Butler has argued that one way to pose the question of who "we" are—who gets to be considered human—is by asking whose lives are mourned and, conversely, whose lives are considered *ungrievable*: "We can see the division of the globe into grievable and ungrievable lives from the perspective of those who wage war in order to defend the lives of certain communities, and to defend them against the lives of others—even if it means taking those latter lives."[2]

Butler understands this distinction to be a political matter. If the value of human life is defined by grievability, then public mourning for lives that have been deemed politically ungrievable can disrupt the hierarchy of political authority. Kavita's dream obliquely indexes two of the more famous examples of this political struggle—the public outrage that was directed at Queen Elizabeth when she initially refused to properly acknowledge Princess Diana's death and the global outrage that ensued after George Floyd was suffocated under the knee of a police officer in Minneapolis. To shift this philosophical language into more familiar terms: what does it mean for lives to matter, and whose lives get to matter?

Kavita's dream directly references the political realities of our racialized social hierarchy. And in sharing it with our research team, she allowed the vision to become something more than a private act of mourning. When the dream was transposed into words and offered to our research team as public testimony, it became an act of reparation.

The power of such statements is hard to overestimate. Our shared belief in the idea of humanity needs to be continuously asserted and reasserted, especially in the aftermath of state-sponsored violence. These cumulative traumas rupture the delicate skin of the social body, undoing the integrity of the idea of a shared human condition. Kavita's testimony shows how dreams can restore these breaches, repairing the injuries to the social fabric by providing new images and new pathways of feelings—*new ways of seeing the world*. Kavita's dream shows us that there are deaths to mourn, there are lives to be acknowledged, and our attachments to one another can be repaired and restored by sharing these visions.

At least this is how it felt to bear witness to Kavita's dream. Listening to the sequence of scenes gave the impression of being surrounded with a bower of images. All the cumulative wounds inflicted during 2020 gave way to the film of this peaceful dream.

After acknowledging the power of what she had shared, our research team asked Kavita what she made of her vision. Here is the wisdom this young woman offered:

> I've been thinking about it, and I think the reason I brought it is because when I woke up, I felt very good. Even though it was some sad stuff going on in the dream—I saw a lot of death, I've just seen someone's funeral. But being able to see a God that I believe in, seeing Princess Diana that I've always looked up to—it was a blessing. My take-home message was about how precious life is. How will I be remembered in this world? What am I doing here? What is my purpose?

Am I meeting my purpose? Is there something I need to change in my life? Do I need to live more happily? What is it that I need to do? Just seeing Princess Diana there, smiling, and happy with her dog. I thought, it's the little things in life, but the most important things. For me, that's what it was about.

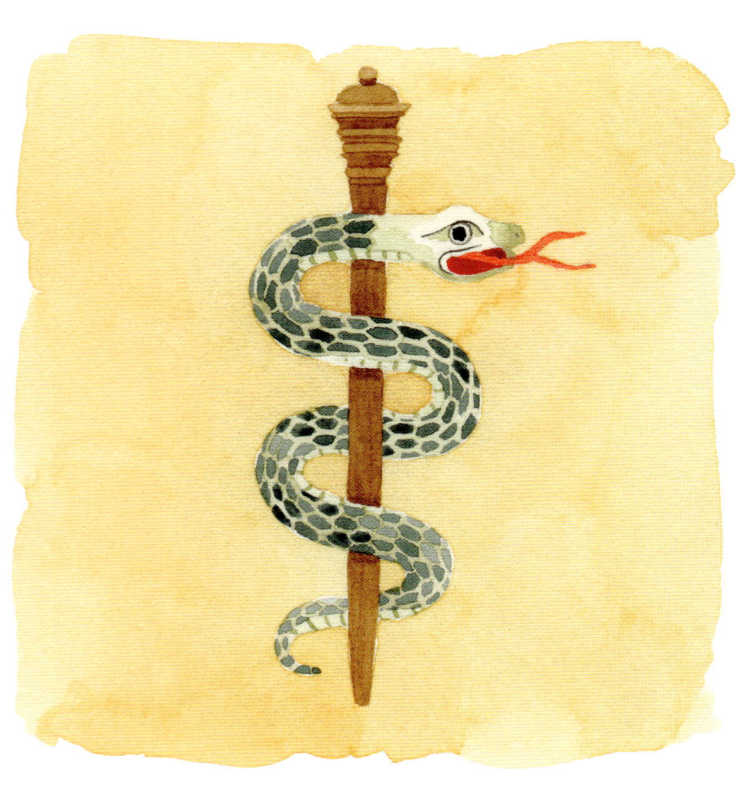

Q IS FOR QUACKERY

One of the more remarkable dreams I've ever heard came from the mother of one of my students. The student's family is Palestinian Christian and moved to Canada from Jordan in the early 2000s. The vision's simplicity adds to its poignancy. In the dream, my student's mother was visited by the Virgin Mary. The saint did not speak but touched the woman lightly on her breast as if to indicate an area of her body that needed attention. When she awoke, she examined her breast and found a lump that later proved to be cancerous.

The dream is extraordinary not only because it alerted the dreamer to a life-threatening illness but also because this information was delivered by a divine figure. To contemporary ears, this might sound miraculous—beyond the grasp of rational thought—but these kinds of visions were once at the center of medical practice.

In ancient Greece, as in many other places, dreams were commonly accepted to have a divine origin, and certain dreams were understood to be direct messages from the gods. The ancient Greek physician Hippocrates was one of the first to propose that these visions could also have a diagnostic purpose. He suggested that dreams could reveal important information about the state of the body.[1]

During Hippocrates's lifetime, the cult of Asclepius, the divine patron of healing, grew, and many temples were established across the region in the doctor-god's name. The asclepieia were important medical sanctuaries for nearly a thousand years—from the fifth century BCE to the late fourth century CE. And the most significant form of treatment at these temples involved incubation (or *enkoimêsis*), a ritual practice of sleeping in a sacred space in hopes of being visited by a dream in which the god would dispense a cure.

From Hippocrates's time through to the height of the Roman empire, Asclepius was the supreme and trusted health adviser, and his main medium of communication was dreams. Even Galen, the famous physician who served several Roman emperors, credited his dreams for many of his diagnoses and for his choice of a medical career. During Galen's life, stories began circulating about a new divine healer whose influence would eventually replace the cult of Asclepius—a young man named Yeshua from Nazareth.[2]

Today, if doctors turned to dreams for a diagnosis, divine or otherwise, they would be labeled quacks. And yet diagnostic dreams persist. In her book *The Committee of Sleep: How Artists, Scientists, and Athletes Use Their Dreams for Creative Problem-Solving—and How You Can Too*, Deirdre Barrett offers several examples of people whose dreams alerted them to spots on their body that turned out to be cancerous. In one case, a man dreamed about a panther who jumped onto his back and clawed him between his shoulder blades. Two months later, his wife found a suspicious mole in the same spot between his shoulder blades. Testing revealed cutaneous melanoma.[3]

One of the few modern doctors who took this function of dreams seriously was Sigmund Freud. Although he is now often remembered for inventing the "talking cure," in his 1917 "A Metapsychological Supplement to the Theory of Dreams," Freud returned to the ancient idea that dreams had a diagnostic function—that is, a particular *way of seeing* the body:

> In dreams, incipient physical disease is often detected earlier and more clearly than in waking life, and all the current bodily sensations assume gigantic proportions. This magnification is hypochondriacal in character; it is conditional upon the withdrawal of all psychical cathexes from the external world back on to the ego, and it makes possible early recognition of bodily changes which in waking life would still for a time have remained unobserved.[4]

Freud is suggesting here that dreams can function like a microscope. This capacity to internally scan the body happens because our perceptual apparatus, which is normally busy with external reality, is turned inward during sleep. The idea is that dreams can work a bit like a CT scan—casting an internal gaze that sweeps the body for symptoms and abnormalities.

Today, many doctors might acknowledge Freud's proposal as an intriguing hypothesis but one that belongs to terrain of psychiatry. Although the modern medical community acknowledges that some ailments have a psychosomatic dimension (they are either caused or aggravated by emotional or environmental stresses), disease is still typically understood to be a separate entity that invades the body. Behind this assumption is the idea that the psyche and the soma are distinct systems. To say that "I have cancer" implies that there is an "I" (a sense of self) that is separate from the cancer (a thing that is not part of the self).[5]

This mechanistic division between mind and body, which is endemic to the Western biomedical model, has received its share of critique over the years. In 1977, the physician George Engel published a now classic paper in the journal *Science* calling for a new biopsychosocial model: "The boundaries between health and disease, between well and sick, are far from clear," he wrote, "and will never be clear because they are affected by cultural, social, and psychological situations."[6] Contemporary physicians such as Gabor Maté have extended this approach to show the interconnection between biology, psychology, and socioeconomic factors.[7]

While the traditional medical model treats disease as having a single cause ("Cigarette smoking causes cancer," according to the US Centers for Disease Control and Prevention), a biopsychosocial approach tries to account for the radical interconnectedness between the emotional centers of the brain, the nervous system, the immune apparatus, and the hormonal organs. Here cancer is understood not just as a malignant change induced by a carcinogen but also as an immune system whose capacity to respond to the abnormality has been diminished by environmental, economic, or emotional stressors.

In a sense, the biopsychosocial approach represents a return to more ancient medical practices. In the asclepieion, the ideas of health and illness were linked to larger questions about community, nature, and the cosmos. The doctors and priests who attended visitors to the sanctuary recognized the importance of patients' attitudes toward their illness and toward the effectiveness of the cure.[8]

To cast this in a slightly different register, a biopsychosocial approach attempts to take into account the *worldliness* of the patient. Here, I am thinking of the Palestinian writer Edward Said's definition of worldliness as *being in the world* and *of the world*.[9] This sense of relationality accounts for the quality of our belonging (or nonbelonging, as the case may be) to culture, class, and community.

Let us return to my student, her mother's dream, and the divine diagnosis. As Said has powerfully articulated, the Palestinian experience has long been one of homelessness. My student's mother and her family are displaced members of a displaced people. The dream is diagnostic in the sense that it addressed the stuff of mortal affairs (it led to a cancer prognosis) but in a way that also attended to the dreamer's spiritual needs. It addressed psyche *and* soma. This is part of what Said meant by worldliness—a recognition of the material realities of being and of the way that geographic, social, and historical forces shape our consciousness, our modes of thought, and our sense of self. The dream carries this worldly optic. Here the dream's radical diagnosis becomes the identification of a malignant tumor but also, simultaneously, an expression of cultural resilience.

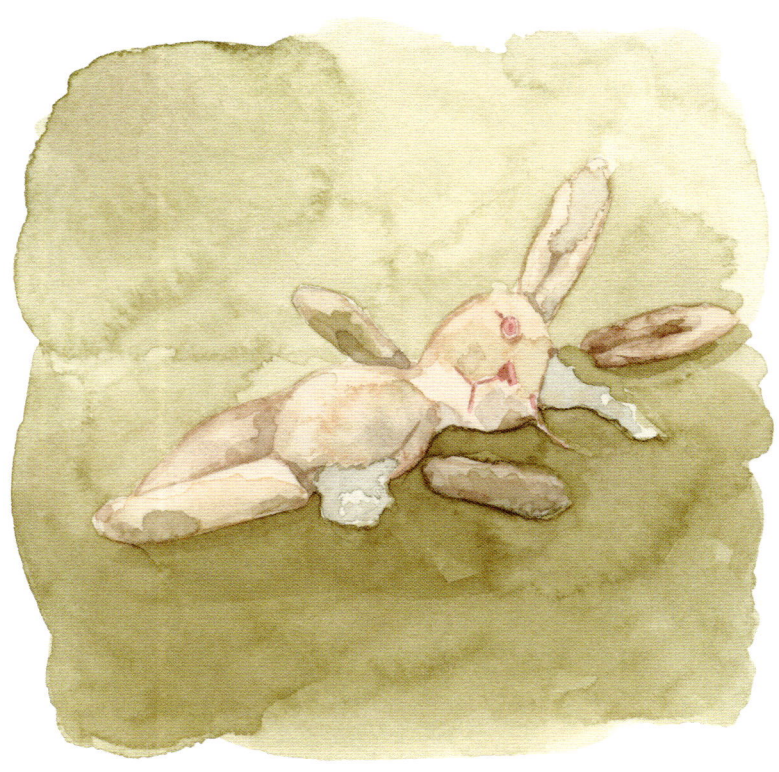

R IS FOR REFUGE

In 2015, during the worst fighting of the Syrian civil war, the Swedish photojournalist Magnus Wennman traveled to Europe and the Middle East to document the plight of refugee children. His resulting photography series, "Where the Children Sleep," depicts a handful of the millions of children whose lives were radically uprooted by an ongoing war that displaced half of Syria's population.[1]

Some of the earliest images Wennman made were in Beirut, Lebanon, where he landed. As he left the airport, the photographer met a Syrian father and his two little girls who were living on the side of a road. They had been sleeping rough for over a year after their home in Damascus was hit by a grenade. "The grenade killed their mother and their brother," Wennman reports: "Now they sleep on a piece of cardboard right next to the road, waiting for cars to stop and throw them some food. Their father told us that every time a car stopped he was afraid that someone would take the kids away from him. He told us that every now and then men in cars asked if they could buy the girls for a few hours."[2]

Apart from documenting where children slept, Wennman also occasionally gathered testimony about the children's dream life. In Belgrade, Serbia, he met five-year-old Abdullah, who was tired and ill. The Syrian boy had been sleeping outside the central station for two days. His mother reported that he was still in shock after witnessing the killing of his sister in their home in Daraa and had nightmares every night.

In another part of Serbia, the photographer encountered five-year-old Lamar. After two attempts to cross the sea from Turkey in a small rubber boat, Lamar and her family eventually reached the Serbian-Hungarian border. Hungarian authorities, however—in defiance of the Geneva Convention, which guarantees refugees the right to seek protection—closed the border with barbed wire and an iron wall, effectively barring access to central Europe. While thousands of refugees camped on the closed motorway near the border, many, like Lamar's family, sought shelter in the nearby forest. Wennman took his picture of Lamar in the early evening on September 15, 2015. In the image, she sleeps wrapped in an Ikea blanket, a few meters away from where her family is resting. Lamar's grandmother told Wennman that the child was with her family when a bomb damaged their house, which prompted the flight. "She dreams of her big dolls, her toy train, and her ball at home in Baghdad. She dreams of a happy life but above all to be able to sleep in a bed again."[3]

One of the few children in the series who slept in a bed is Fatima, who was nine when Wennman photographed her in Sweden. Fatima and her mother and siblings fled from their home in Idlib when the Syrian national army began slaughtering civilians in the city. After two years in a Lebanese refugee camp, the family made its way to Libya and boarded an overcrowded boat to cross the Mediterranean. After sailing for twelve hours in the brutally hot sun, a fellow passenger gave birth to a still-born baby on the deck of the boat, and as Fatima watched, two men threw the infant into the sea.

The refugees were finally rescued by the Italian coastguard when their boat started to take on water. Fatima's family reached safety in Europe, eventually settling in Norberg, Sweden. Despite this relative safety, every night Fatima dreams that she is falling from a ship. The photographer led his caption with this fact, encouraging his viewers to envisage this *other scene* that is not available to our gaze:

> Every night, Fatima dreams that she's falling from a ship. Together with her mother, Malaki, and her two siblings, Fatima fled from the city Idlib when the Syrian national army senselessly slaughtered civilians in the city. After two years in a refugee camp in Lebanon, the situation became

unbearable and they made it to Libya where they boarded an overcrowded boat. On the deck of the boat, a very pregnant woman gave birth to her baby after twelve hours in the scorching sun. The baby was a stillbirth and was thrown overboard. Fatima saw everything. When the refugee's boat started to take on water, they were picked up by the Italian coastguard.

Wennman's series belongs squarely within the documentary genre. The project is designed to animate our collective sense of social concern. Although we may be wary of the way the photographs frame reality, these images are generally accepted as evidence of a handful of children's experiences of the Syrian war. We might even applaud the photographer's effort to document these scenes—enabling the world to *see* and therefore *know* something of what these young refugees have gone through. But as Christina Sharpe reminds us, "spectacle is not repair."[4]

The problem with this way of seeing has to do with the structure of the exchange between the viewer (us) and the subject (the children). As Martha Rosler once put it: "Documentary photography carries (old) information about a group of powerless people to another group addressed as socially powerful."[5] Under the guise of journalistic objectivity, these photographs seize a particular moment of suffering in order to awaken concern in the viewer. But there is temporal a sleight of hand involved in this exchange: the moment that the photograph depicts is discontinuous with the time in which it is viewed. And as many critics have argued, this temporal discontinuity actively works to depoliticize the reality it purports to represent. "The picture becomes evidence of the general human condition," John Berger argued: "It accuses nobody and everybody."[6] Although Wennman's photographs seem to deliver information about these causalities of the Syrian war, the cause of this suffering is not pictured. And this can accelerate the naturalization of the political condition that these children face. Viewers of the photographs are led to assume that the status of refugee is an inadvertent outcome of civil war rather than the deliberate goal of our contemporary global order.

Despite the various declarations and treaties crafted after the Second World War—which officially acknowledge our collective obligation to provide safe and secure conditions for refugees, migrants, and other displaced people—governments around the world are inventing new ways to strip people of their political personhood on a scale heretofore unimaginable. According to the UN Refugee Agency's latest numbers, more than 117 million people have been forcibly displaced or became stateless by 2023—a number that has been increasing exponentially since 2011, when the Syrian war began.[7] These refugees are made stateless not when they lose their citizenship but when the countries from whom they seek refuge deliberately bar entry, often for the things supposedly protected by universal human rights—race, ethnicity, or religion. This is happening at international borders around the world. Hannah Arendt's chilling observation about the Second World War is even more true today: "the world [finds] nothing sacred in the abstract nakedness of being human."[8]

These children know what it means to teeter on the precipice of life. Their testimony issues a call that far exceeds the familiar liberal demand for recognition of their right to become citizens of a new polity. We need another way of seeing what is happening, and we need a more imaginative response against fortified borders and political machinations that deny dignity to these children.

The etymology of the word *imagination* might be instructive here. Imagination involves the capacity to form mental images (*imagos* in Latin) and the capacity to represent them to oneself. This concept can also refer to the individual cognitive process that shapes our perception and the social forces that structure and authorize our systems of knowledge and modes of belonging—the frames of the social imaginary that structure our collective ways of seeing.

If documentary risks becoming spectacle, what might a reparative frame look like? The photographer himself provides a path to this other way of seeing. In his captions, Magnus Wennman notes that many of these refugee children have vivid nightmares. What if we privileged these testimonies, this other way of seeing? What do these dreams manage to say or rather *show* that is not legible to the documentary tradition? What might be gained by granting these nightmares a proper hearing? What if we listened to what the children themselves report rather than subjecting their wretched situations to our gaze? A dream, after all, is an exercise of our fundamental capacity to form new images in the mind. Taking these other visions seriously as an equally important form of evidence might allow us to register this political crisis differently and to better grasp what it means to fall into the void of statelessness.

Shortly after his series, *Where the Children Sleep*, was published (and subsequently won international acclaim), Wennman granted one of the children's experience a larger hearing in a short film called *Fatima's Drawings*. The five-minute film follows nine-year-old Fatima as she travels from her new house in Sweden to school and back home again. Spectators sit with her as she quietly draws with colored pencils at a kitchen table on a gray day. We listen as she describes her former life in Syria, playing with her friend Rana, seeing the planes and bombs that destroyed her home, and witnessing the incident that haunts her dreams:

> When we took the big boat, there was a mother who gave birth to a baby—a girl or a boy, I don't know. Then I watched as two men threw the baby into the sea. It was the first time I saw something like that. It was not good. I do not like the sea. (03:36–4:35)

The film adds subtle animation to Fatima's drawing of the big boat. We watch as she adds a few lines to one of the figures on the boat and then drops her pencil and leaves the frame. The camera stays with the drawing, moving closer to take in the details. The boat begins to bob gently on the water the child has drawn. The sun moves across the sky as the tiny baby slowly falls into the sea. The film closes with Fatima in bed, clutching her teddy bear, expressing a wish to be able to play with Rana again.[9]

Wennman's film allows Fatima to present her experience largely on her own terms and, by focusing on her drawings, raises questions about what kind of knowledge these differing forms of testimony provide—oral, visual, and oneiric. *Fatima's Drawings* offers a different view of the war crimes occurring in Syria—a conflict that some international investigators have described as a "war on children."[10]

One of the great paradoxes of the category of violence we call war crimes or crimes against humanity is that this violence often includes a secondary form of damage: beyond the physical destruction, these crimes can also deprive their victims of the ability to speak about what occurred. This can happen when a testifying statement is deprived of its authority or when victims are rendered expressionless. As the philosopher Jean-François Lyotard has noted, in addition to the suffering constituted by the damage itself, "there is added the impossibility of bringing it to the knowledge of others, and in particular the knowledge of a tribunal."[11] In Fatima's case, this young refugee was exposed to a form of violence that destroyed her home, killed members of her family, and more insidiously, wounded her ability to consciously share her experience with others.

An important part of the work of international tribunals is to find a way to help such witnesses come to expression, to facilitate the sharing of their experience, and to lend legitimacy to these expressions through a formal hearing. This process can have a powerful reparative function. The capacity to share one's experience with others is a vital human strategy that can help to sustain a sense of agency in the face of disempowering circumstances. The reconstitution of events in the form of a narrative involves actively reworking the events and no longer living them in passivity. The court's processes transform private experiences into public meaning and can work to reinvent the definition of the human community, authorizing notions of who we are and the ties that hold us together. Attending to this testimony, in turn, calls into being an imagined community that recognizes that what needs to be communicated often exceeds what can be presently phrased.

When Fatima speaks of what she witnessed on the "big boat," she is at a loss for words and is able only to report: "It was the first time I saw something like that. It was not good." What happens in this moment when Fatima's verbal account falters? How are we to understand what she means by "that" ("It was the first time I saw something like that") without saying it points to something that exceeds her capacity to narrate, a lack in her command of the language? Fatima's use of the demonstrative pronoun refers to an experience that undoubtedly carries great force and that no words might be adequate to express. Even the greatest storytellers struggle to articulate their experience of statelessness. As Stefan Zweig once said of the "cruel condition," it is hard to explain to anyone who has not known it themselves: "It is a nerve-racking sense of teetering on the brink, wide awake and staring into nothing, knowing that wherever you find a foothold you can be thrust back into the void at any moment."[12]

For Fatima, the paralyzing sight of men throwing a dead baby into the sea—an experience that she refers to as "that"—seems to serve as a marker of this primal void. What better representation could there be for the terrible precariousness of statelessness? This condition involves not only a loss of citizenship but also the experience of being stripped of personhood—cast out of the sphere of human recognition altogether. In her recurring dream, Fatima finds herself falling from the ship, as though spellbound in a moment of identification with the infant who was thrown overboard like garbage. This child's nightmare is a perfect testament—if ever there could be one—to what it means to be reduced to the condition of bare life.

But where there is a dream, there is hope. Fatima's awful nightmare represents one of the direst conflicts of our times with acute clarity. This mental image produced *in* the condition of statelessness becomes a powerful image *of* this condition. Listening to this testimony, we might begin to understand how a child's dream can become a remarkably effective diagnostic tool—a prevision of a political history in the process of becoming.[13] By sharing this dream, Fatima transposed private angst into a public thing, material from which the social fabric might be woven anew. For those of us lucky enough not to find ourselves facing such circumstances, our task is to exercise our own imagination—to *attend* these visions in a way that creates new spaces of refuge.

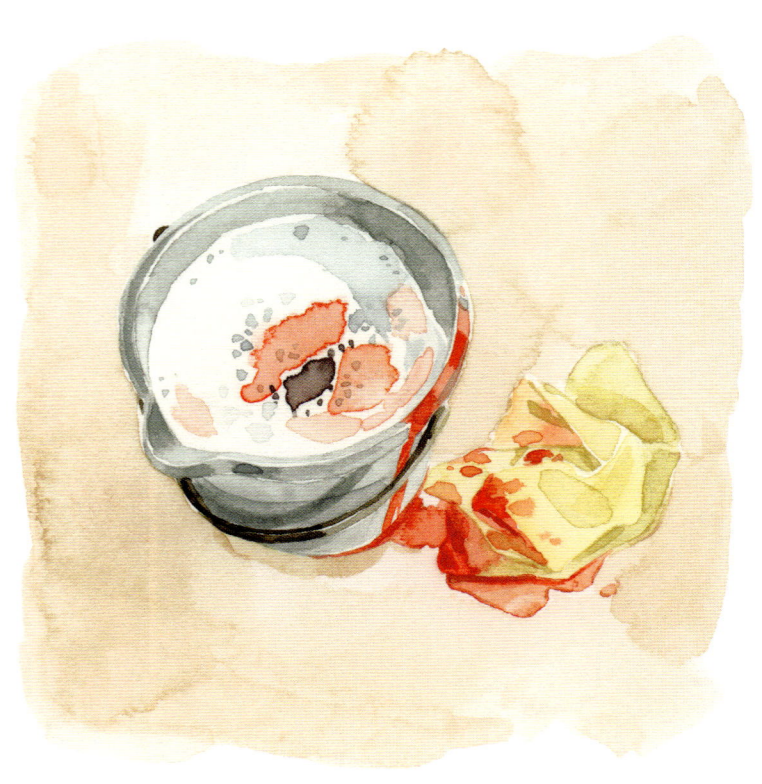

S IS FOR SUICIDE

When one finds oneself existing in a reality that is designed to be unlivable, the pressure of this disjointed state—being alive in a world that seems to want you dead—can be unbearable. In these moments, the freedom offered by nonexistence can feel enticing. It is hard to describe this feeling state without romanticizing suicide or pathologizing it.

Billy-Ray Belcourt uses the phrase "contorted living" to describe this feeling-state. Belcourt is a poet who is attuned to the resonances of language and he had the Attawapiskat First Nation in mind when he used this particular phrase. On April 9, 2016, this small community, which is situated at the mouth of the Attawapiskat River on James Bay in Northern Ontario, declared a state of emergency when eleven residents attempted suicide on a single day. Belcourt, who is a member of the Driftpile Cree nation, wrote a poem for these residents—or rather, he wrote *to* them—and then deleted it from his first book, a poetry collection titled *This Wound Is a World*.[1] He again tried to say something about the situation, and this piece eventually became the basis for an essay that appears in his third book, *A History of My Brief Body*.

Belcourt articulates how the sense of unlivability can be produced by external forces and how this manufactured feeling can seep into the self, creating a disequilibrium that people feel in their innermost core. The poet is especially attentive to the ways that Canada has fostered a climate of unlivability for Indigenous peoples, creating a pervasive climate of exhaustion through a combination of genocidal violence and institutional neglect: "There's dizzying evidence of the unlivability of Canada wherever one looks. That NDN kids, NDN women and men, queers and trans NDNs are all enticed by the freedom of nonexistence is an ethical problem at the core of Canadian modernity."[2] Nation states deliberately manufacture sorrow for some of their citizens, and Canada is a country that is built on the suppression of Indigenous vitality.

But Belcourt does more than articulate what it feels like to be "in the throes of a genocide." He also calls for and then delivers "a new grammar of living," offering a vibrant language for choosing to live despite such conditions.[3] Belcourt writes from the side of joy and refuses to position this choice in opposition to the choice to die. (As Sakue Shimohira notes, some environments can be so unlivable that they require different kinds of courage—the courage to die and the courage to live.)[4] In such contexts, suicide emerges as a political response to structurally manufactured despair. Poetry, for Belcourt, is a way develop a deeper understanding of why some people choose death, and a practice of "radical empathy for those who experience aliveness as a kind of everpresent death knell."[5] Like Audre Lorde, Belcourt understands poetry to be a survival tactic, a practice that helps people stay on the side of life.

I have learned a great deal from Belcourt's work. His writing has offered me a way to understand a feeling that I knew intimately but had no words for. Let me be clear: as a white person who grew up in the settler colonial nation that is Canada, I do not know what it feels like to exist in a nation that constantly deploys strategies designed to eradicate my existence. In fact, my country's violence is enacted on Indigenous life precisely to *make space* for people like me, a child of two white immigrants. And at times, my complicity with my country's system of whiteness means that I, too, have deployed this form of violence in a "mirror-register"—by retreating into naïveté, by claiming to speak in the universal, by lapsing into defensiveness, by resorting to silence.[6]

The place where I feel a strong kinship with Belcourt is in his descriptions of how living in a queer body can also feel like an impossible undertaking. I grew up in a social world that treated my behavior, my carriage, my clothing, my voice, and especially my sexuality as "nonconforming." I learned to avoid certain spaces where I might encounter people who were intent on policing this perceived nonconformity (or worse). In this respect, I intimately identified with Belcourt's description of "contorted living."

In my case, the most intense form of violence I experienced came from my immediate family. When I was about twenty-one, my father declared me dead: "There is a spiteful lesbian living somewhere in Toronto," he wrote at the end of one of his typewritten letters, "but my little girl is dead to me." It was generally agreed that my father's handwriting was impossible to read, but nevertheless, his use of a typewriter in this case seemed to carry its own, secondary message. The bitterness he felt toward me prevented him from extending any intimacy— even the tenuous amity of his handwriting.

For a long time, I stored my father's letters in a metal box, as if the solidity of the metal could protect me from them. I knew this was irrational, but I found it difficult even to touch the envelopes in which his letters arrived. They felt like the magical devices that appear in ancient tragedies—like the poisoned dress Medea sends to her treacherous husband's new bride-to-be, a garment that Euripides describes as being infused with a "devouring fire" that melts the flesh off the young woman's bones, leaving her limbs "weeping like pine resin."[7] The ancients understood unreason. They knew that wrath could manifest.

In my early twenties, I moved to Toronto in hopes the city would offer respite from the overwhelming sense of unliveability. But one day, for reasons I still cannot fully explain, I found myself standing on the wrong side of the thick yellow safety line that is painted on subway platforms. I had no intention of boarding the next train. I think some part of me had accepted my father's death sentence and I felt that it was up to me to carry out his judgment—I had become my own executioner.

Around this time, I started having a recurring nightmare. The first version of the nightmare featured our family dog, a nervous Labrador retriever named Annie, which I had begged my parents to adopt a year before I left for university. In the dream, the dog and I were jumping and chasing each other playfully. Then Annie turned a corner sharply and suddenly her body split in half spewing blood and guts as if torn apart by an invisible giant. In the rest of the nightmare, I found myself weeping uncontrollably on my knees, as if in supplication, mopping up my dog's guts with a bucket and rag.

In another version of the dream, I find myself standing in a field looking up into a blue sky, watching a propeller plane do lazy loop-de-loops. It is a thrilling, joyful sight. The plane moves effortlessly through the sky, defying the laws of gravity. Suddenly, it loses momentum and begins a terrifying, spiraling nosedive toward the ground. I do not see the crash, but I can hear it and see smoke rising in the distance. I sprint across the field, and as I approach the smoking wreckage, I find the pilot lying face down trying to push himself up from the ground. He does not seem to realize that he has been severed in half at the waist. I can still recall the feeling of frozen terror as he looked up at me, bewildered about why he couldn't get purchase amid the slippery mess of guts under his chest.

This type of nightmare rarely visits me now. But when it does, the central elements are always the same. Someone is suddenly, violently split in half, and I find myself alone and helpless, forced to witness the scene, and simultaneously responsible for dealing with the terrible aftermath.

It took many years for me to realize that my nightmares were both dramatizing my situation—*showing me* what I had, in fact, experienced—*and* keeping me on the side of life. Dreams animate life. That is their work. Like the poet's labor, these productions work to vivify our experience—and especially the kinds of experiences that run counter to the prevailing social orders in which we struggle to exist: "beauty as a troubling of normality," as Belcourt puts it.[8]

Sigmund Freud would probably diagnose my dream as a symptom of "splitting." This is his description of the way that the ego can rupture in response to a traumatic situation, leading to the coexistence, within a single subject, of "two different attitudes, contrary to and independent of each other."[9] Freud was puzzled by the fact that often no compromise is made to resolve these divisions within the self. The fissure simply remains a fissure, which, he admits, "almost deserves to be described as artful" in its response to a traumatic reality.[10]

My nightmare, like my conscious experience of my father's death decree, continues to be devastating. Part of me is devastated anew every time the nightmare comes. Part of me is never not devastated. But the dream also, simultaneously, reveals that a radical remaking of the world is possible. It is a revelation, in the fullest sense of the word—a call to choose life.

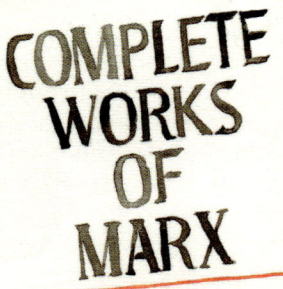

COMPLETE WORKS OF MARX

including
the poetry

Edited by
PAUL B. PRECIADO

T IS FOR TRANS

Paul B. Preciado knew that choosing a new name was going to be a political matter. When he started experimenting with small doses of testosterone in 2004, he kept his birth name, Beatriz, which he understood to be neither male nor female. He asked his friends and colleagues at the Barcelona Museum of Contemporary Art to continue to call him Beatriz but to use male pronouns. But this "grammatical torsion"—keeping a feminine name while using masculine pronouns—proved even more difficult that the corporeal fluidity of his gender.[1]

After years of living in "the nameless space between female and male," Paul decided to renounce fluidity—paradoxically, because he wanted change.[2] And so he chose to cross the binary to see what was on the other side.

According to his own account, choosing a new name proved to be "a crazy adventure." He asked his friends to look for names, but the names they wanted (Orlando, Max, Pascal) were impossible: "They meant too much for them and were too difficult to carry; it was too much responsibility."[3] Beatriz turned to a shaman and participated in a series of rituals designed to invoke a new name. The shaman said Beatriz's name would come to him in his dreams. After completing the rituals, Preciado went to sleep, but no great revelation arrived. Weeks later, just as he had begun to forget about the shaman's pronouncement, on an ordinary night in December 2015, he experienced what he calls a "strong dream":

> In it, a publishing house found the secret poetry of Marx. I offered to edit the work and written on the cover of the book was "Complete works of Marx including the poetry, edited by Paul B. Preciado." I woke up and called the shaman. She said, "It's your name," and I accepted. It was disrupting, but beautiful.[4]

And so Preciado accepted the "strange, absurdly commonplace" name that came to him in a dream[5] and began asking everyone to call him Paul. He also began the legal process to officially change his name and "sex" (gender) with the state. With the help of his lawyer, Preciado formally requested the Spanish government to recognize him as a man. The decision was handed down in November 2016, and ever since, the influential writer, curator, and activist has been known as Paul B. Preciado.

The journey of gender transition is marked by a series of borders. Preciado's book, *An Apartment on Uranus: Chronicles of the Crossing* (the title comes from another dream), chronicles his experience of this crossing, which involves much more than navigating medical and legal systems. Throughout the journey, he intimately comes to understand the ways that the sex and gender binary has become one of the "most violent of political borders invented by humanity."[6]

To be trans, according to Preciado, means embracing change and accepting the idea that one becomes oneself only through metamorphosis. In contrast, the hetero-patriarchal system of sexual difference rests on a lethal insistence that human beings are *immutable*. This system is built on the idea that one is born either male or female, ignoring the complex and diverse array of gender expression in favor of a false colonial binary. The border between these two categories is defined as an irrevocable fact and policed accordingly. Those who attempt to cross this border are often deemed psychotic and treated as enemies of the system. Children who are born with a noticeable variation in their anatomy (intersex people, for instance, who have "indeterminate" genitals) are often subjected to nonconsensual and medically unnecessary surgical operations designed to conform their bodies to one or the other sex (gender).

As trans discourse proliferates and as more people understand the border between male and female to be porous, efforts to police this binary system have grown. Violence against trans people has increased exponentially. Even as officials have started acknowledging the murders of trans people in the United States, the numbers have escalated. Black, Brown, and Indigenous trans women are disproportionally targeted. This lethal violence is both tacitly and explicitly sanctioned by governmental officials who have sought to politicize the sex and gender border for their own ends. The number of US legislative bills discriminating against trans people has broken records over four consecutive years. In 2023, an unprecedented number of bills were introduced across health care, athletics, the military, incarceration, and education. Even more bills were introduced in 2024, and on his first day back in office in 2025, President Trump issued a raft of policies targeting transgender Americans.[7]

Change is an integral part of life. To insist that there are only two immutable sexes is at odds with contemporary scientific knowledge, which provides evidence of a startling variety of anatomical, chromosomal, and hormonal combinations of biological sexual characteristics. This insistence also goes against the grain of human history, which is filled with stories of individuals who have undertaken the crossing and cultures that are not governed by a pernicious binary but revere the mutability of gender.

We all have access to this school of metamorphosis in our dreams. As Paul B. Preciado himself puts it: "the human psyche never stops creating and dealing with reality, sometimes in dreams, sometimes in waking life."[8]

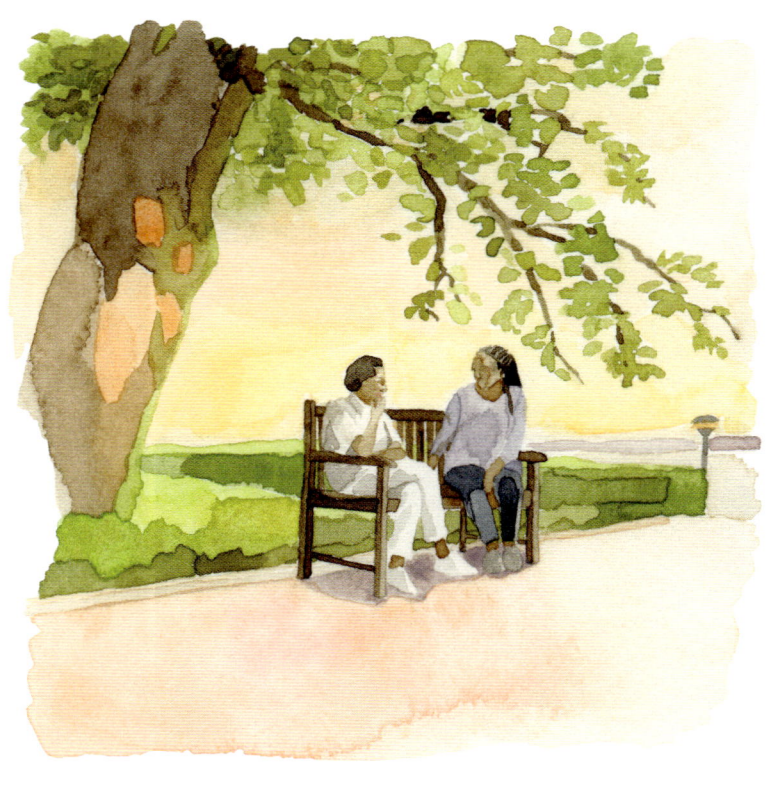

U IS FOR UTOPIA

I am embarrassed to admit that I only recently became familiar with Octavia Butler's work. I studied English literature at university in the 1990s, and her novel *Parable of the Sower* was widely discussed at the time, but I have always struggled with the genre of science fiction.

When I finally did start reading Butler, I found I couldn't stop. Over one summer, I devoured the entirety of her oeuvre—twelve novels and a short story collection—and the source of my block became clear. Before Butler, I thought that all science fiction portrayed future worlds that were replete with the same oppressions that make the present so unlivable—imperialism, patriarchy, white supremacy, militarized violence, and climate crisis. Often these oppressions are just enlarged to a galactic scale.

As commentators have noted, Octavia Butler took on many of these issues but "with the arc always bending towards justice." She was part of a generation of writers that birthed a unique kind of "visionary fiction," a form that encompasses all the fantastic elements of science fiction but in a way that aims to decolonize the imagination.[1] In Butler's hands, science fiction becomes a kind of political *praxis*, a means to try out possible futures that bend toward justice.

Like many science fiction novels from the latter half of the twentieth century, the protagonists of Butler's fiction face a series of challenges, including alien encounters (the Xeno-genesis trilogy), an extraterrestrial plague (the Patternist series), and political authoritarianism meets climate collapse (the Parable series). But unlike many science fiction novels, Butler's protagonists are almost always Black women. And despite facing familiar forms of oppression, these characters usually become reluctant leaders who can remain attentive to an inner truth that guides their efforts toward social transformation.

One of Butler's most compactly illustrative stories in this respect is called "The Book of Martha."[2] First published online in 2003, the short story's framing structure is simple: God appears to the titular character and tasks her with coming up with an idea to improve humanity. Butler provides readers with access to the protagonist's thoughts, so we follow Martha as she processes the weight of the assignment.

At first, God appears as a living version of Michelangelo's *Moses*, a sculpture Martha recalls seeing in an art history textbook. When she questions God about his appearance, he replies: "You see what your life has prepared you to see." As the conversation continues, God changes form, first into a normal-sized white man, then into a Black man, and finally into a Black woman who resembles Martha herself. Even God is not aware of these shifting appearances. The transformations provide a lesson in how expectations influence perception—and how liberating it feels to become aware of this fact.[3]

God's task for Martha is to "help humankind to survive its greedy, murderous, wasteful adolescence. Help it to find less destructive, more peaceful, sustainable ways to live."[4] She must decide on one change that will transform the character of humanity for the better. At first Martha is terrified about the overwhelming nature of the task and wants to go home. Then she worries about making a mistake. Eventually, she begins to ponder the labor in earnest, asking herself, "what if she were going to write a novel in which human beings had to be changed in only one positive way?"[5] (Martha, like Butler, is a novelist, and she uses her professional skills to think through the task.) The conversation continues as Martha tries out ideas and God warns her about unintended consequences. The significance of the story's title becomes clear when Martha recalls similar stressful encounters between God and figures from the Bible.

Martha finally settles on an idea: people should have "powerful, unavoidable, realistic dreams that come every single time people sleep." Her thinking behind this is twofold: the dreams will fulfill deep-seated desires in a virtual way, but they will also promote more thoughtfulness and concern for real consequences in waking life. The dreams will push people "toward some kind of waking maturity," which will help them grow "less susceptible to lies, peer pressure, and self-delusion."[6]

The direct simplicity of Butler's proposal never fails to astonish me: Martha's plan to improve the character humanity involves learning from our dreams. She recognizes that our need for fantasy is indispensable—we need a place where our wildest desires can be nurtured and fulfilled—but we also need to grow our awareness in waking life. Dreams provide both.

In an afterword, Butler offers a brief commentary on her short story. She describes "The Book of Martha" as "her utopian story" and admits that most utopian stories are unbelievable: "It seems inevitable that my utopia would be someone else's hell." In a handful of pages, Butler deals with all the major scholarly quarrels with this complicated concept.[7]

The word *utopia* was coined by Thomas More in 1516 as a kind of joke. In Latin, the word means "no place." And even today, the idea of utopia is often thought to be escapist nonsense: a perfect world is a good fantasy but is practically impossible to achieve. Centuries of debate on the concept of utopia have tended to fall into two broad schools. A liberal and humanist tradition tends to focus on the question of form (a long literary tradition explores what a good society might look like), and a Marxist tradition defines utopia in terms of its function (here the focus is on what facilitates the education of desire or, conversely, what prevents social change). In a way, these two sides of the debate distinguish between the concrete and abstract expressions of the concept of utopia.[8]

In "The Book of Martha," Butler's character quickly recognizes that everyone has a different idea of perfection, which makes God's task seemingly impossible. But she does not give up. Like her Biblical counterparts, Martha accepts the unwelcome burden and grapples with her own complicated desire to find a better way of being. The character acknowledges the extent of people's sense of alienation, which makes space for the desire for a better world to be both realistic *and* unrealistic. And by turning to dreams, Martha lands on a solution that can accommodate the fact that the idea of utopia is both individualistic and changeable over time.

"The Book of Martha" is not the first time Butler used dreams in her work. At the beginning of *Parable of the Sower*, the fifteen-year-old protagonist, Lauren Oya Olamina, has a dream that foreshadows the novel's events and sets the seeds for her burgeoning system of belief, which she calls Earthseed. Like many of the most significant figures from history, this character allows herself to be guided by the visions that come to her under the cover of sleep, tapping into the precognitive potential that lies in this dimension.

Many of Butler's own visions have already come to pass. *Parable of the Sower* (published in 1993) opens in Los Angeles in 2024 at a time when global warming has brought rising seawater and increasing drought. Pharmaceutical companies have created a series of drugs that enthrall the population. Trust in the police is at an all-time low. And a presidential candidate promises to "Make America Great Again."

Regardless of whether the novel is a cautionary tale or a prophecy, one of the most important lessons Octavia Butler bequeathed to us is that we must be brave enough to imagine beyond the seemingly intractable boundaries of our existing world. And dreams are a crucial tool for this work.

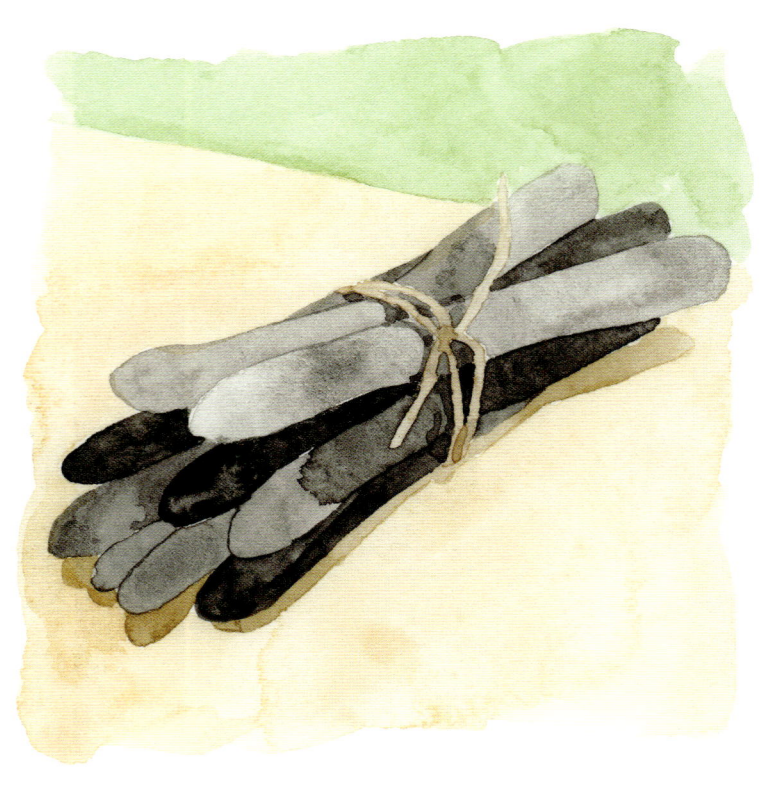

V IS FOR VEGETABLES

Some dreams open a space where rational understanding cannot penetrate. Sometimes these dreams remain perplexingly enigmatic, and sometimes their significance becomes clear over time.

Among the many dreams that appear in Sigmund Freud's *Interpretation of Dreams*, one of easiest to overlook is called the market dream. Freud spends relatively little time with this dream. He notes that it comes from one of his patients, an anonymous young woman whom he identifies as "intelligent and cultivated" but reserved and shy in her behavior. The woman related the following dream:

> I dreamt that I went to the market with my cook, but we arrived too late to get anything. The butcher didn't have what I asked for. He offered me something else, but I rejected it and went on to the woman who sells vegetables. She tried to get me to buy a particular vegetable that was tied up lengthwise in bundles but was of a black colour. I said: "I don't recognize that; I won't take it."[1]

Freud informs readers that the content of the dream is directly related to events from the prior day. The young woman had, in fact, gone to the market and arrived too late to buy anything. But while the dream appears unmemorable, the experience it testifies to is anything but banal. As the dreamer followed the chain of her associations—giving voice to all the stray thoughts and images that came to her mind as she considered each part of her dream—a path to the source of the dream eventually became accessible.

Freud shares some of the woman's associations in his book. We learn, for instance, that the phrases spoken in the dream came directly from real-life events, including a dispute the dreamer had with her cook the day before, in which she admonished his behavior: "I don't recognize that! Behave yourself properly!" The image of the long black vegetables tied up in bundles recalled the idea of male genitals. (No association to the black color was recorded.[2]) And as the woman continued to speak of her dream, she said (in German), "The meat shop was closed." Freud notes that the phrase is a striking echo of a much more vulgar one: "Your meat shop's open" ("Du hast deine Fleischbank offen"), which is Viennese slang for "Your fly is undone."

Apart from noting these sexual overtones, Freud does not offer an interpretation of the dream. After describing the direct connection between the elements of the dream and the woman's day, he moves on to other topics and other dreams.

A decade later, when a subsequent edition of the *Interpretation of Dreams* was published, Freud quietly returned to this dream. In a footnote added in 1909, the doctor reveals that the market dream occurred at the beginning of the patient's treatment. Much later, Freud realized that the dream was a vehicle through which this shy young woman was able to return to the initial trauma that brought her into treatment—a sexual assault in her childhood. In the footnote, Freud suggests the dream seeks "to bring about a repetition" of the trauma.[3] It seems that even as an adult, this woman was still trying to find words for what had happened to her as a child. The dream borrowed events that occurred during the day—a trip to the market, a fight with her cook—to restage this childhood encounter in her internal theater. At some level, the woman made an association between these two experiences, creating a link between what happened at the market and what happened during her childhood assault ("Here we go again: I am being presented with something I do not want").

What is astonishing to me is that in the imaginary theater of her dream, this shy young woman returned to this impactful scene in order to *refuse* what was on offer: "No, I will not take that," she said to herself. This radical gesture of refusal was made possible by the act of restaging of this scene from the past.

In the landscape of dream life, an ordinary, everyday encounter at the market becomes material through which a traumatic experience from childhood can be revisited. Beyond simply returning the dreamer to the scene of this encounter—bringing about a "repetition" of it, as Freud suggested—the dream provided the possibility for its *transformation*. The memory of a childhood sexual assault was transfigured into a drama of resistance and refusal.

It is such a simple thing, this dream of going to the market—a minor gesture, the smallest of experimental acts. And yet it allowed the dreamer to restage and revise a wounding childhood event, and in so doing, shift the moorings of her being.

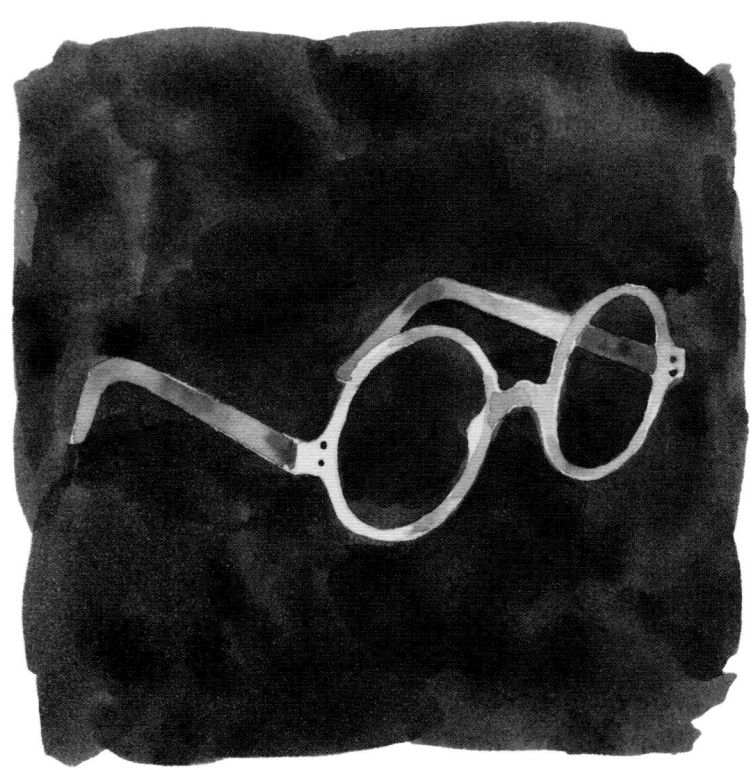

W IS FOR WHITE WOLVES

One of the most famous dreams in the annals of medical science is the childhood nightmare of Sergei Pankejeff.[1] Pankejeff was born into a wealthy Russian family in 1886. As a young man, he suffered from a debilitating depression among other symptoms, and after spending time in a variety of European hospitals, he traveled to Vienna to see Dr. Freud.

A great deal has been written about Pankejeff, beginning in 1918 with the publication of Freud's case study "From the History of an Infantile Neurosis."[2] The sensational nature of the case inspired a profusion of commentary from practitioners and scholars. Freud's presentation of Pankejeff's case reads like a novel, inviting interpretation, which the doctor delivers in spectacular fashion. But apart from its sensational quality, the case is unique in that, at age eighty-three, Pankejeff himself published a memoir that included his own recollections of Freud. This is a rare instance in which the patient looked back, so to speak, reversing the medical gaze.

The vast cornucopia of materials about "the Wolf Man," as Pankejeff came to be known, is impossible to summarize here, but the dream that sparked these responses is relatively simple. In his first week of treatment with Freud, Pankejeff shared a childhood nightmare, and over four years of analysis, the dream gradually became a kind of keystone—a marker of where the patient's neurosis began (in Freud's view) but also the focus of much subsequent interpretation.

As reported in Freud's case study, Pankejeff had this dream on the eve of his fourth birthday in 1890:

I dreamt that it was night and that I was lying in bed. (My bed stood with its foot towards the window; in front the window there was a row of old walnut trees. I know it was winter time when I had the dream, and night-time.) Suddenly the window opened of its own accord, and I was terrified to see that some white wolves were sitting on the big walnut tree in front of the window. There were six or seven of them. The wolves were quite white, and looked more like foxes or sheep dogs, for they had big tails like foxes and they had their ears pricked like dogs when they are attending to something. In great terror, evidently of being eaten up by the wolves, I screamed and woke up.[3]

Pankejeff also provided a drawing of his dream, which Freud included in the published his case history, and over the years, he painted and repainted the image.

Elements of this infamous dream are easily traced to Pankejeff's social world, including the large estate on which he grew up north of the city of Kherson (which now lies within the borders of Ukraine). The estate was large enough to host country fairs, and in his memoir, Pankejeff recalls peeking through the garden gate at the lively scene of a Romani horse market, where "gypsies and other strange people" gathered around campfires, shouting and gesticulating wildly as they negotiated their sales.[4]

Apart from growing crops, the estate also raised sheep. One year, Pankejeff remembers, a dangerous epidemic broke out. All the animals that remained healthy—some 200,000 sheep— were inoculated, but by some accident or purposeful villainy, the wrong serum was delivered, and all the inoculated sheep died catastrophically. Pankejeff's father then bought a second estate further north in a region full of "primeval forests." Every summer, the peasants from adjacent villages organized a wolf hunt that ended with a festive evening of folk music and dancing hosted by Sergei's father.

In his early childhood, Pankejeff and his elder sister, Anna, were cared for by a nurse, Nanya, as well as a succession of governesses, tutors, and servants. Pankejeff recalls that one of these figures, an English governess called Miss Oven, enjoyed sadistically teasing young Sergei. Her "harmful" influence produced a change in the child's character around the time of the dream. Once "quiet, and almost phlegmatic," Pankejeff became "a very nervous, irritable child subject to severe temper tantrums."[5]

After Miss Oven was dismissed, a new Bulgarian governess named Miss Elisabeth joined the household. Pankejeff recalls that she smoked cigarettes all day long and frequently spoke of the atrocities the Bulgarians suffered at the hands of the Turks (during the Russian-Turkish war). In the evening, Miss Elisabeth would read to the children. The reading matter consisted almost entirely of Russian translations of Grimms' *Fairy Tales*, and Pankejeff recalls being particularly terrified of an illustration of a wolf standing on its hind legs from the story of "Little Red Riding Hood." Sergei's elder sister, Anna, contrived occasions to surprise her brother with this picture, which would invariably produce emotional outbursts.

Anna was two years older than her brother. In his memoir, Sergei describes a "very deep, personal, inner relationship" with his sister, whom he considered his "only comrade."[6] In his case study, Freud reports that while they were still very young children, Anna had "seduced" her younger brother into "sexual practices." On one occasion, she "took hold of his penis and played with it." On another, occasion she suggested they "show each other their bottoms."[7] Subsequent research into the household suggests that Anna's sexual precocity stemmed from having herself been the subject of a sexual "seduction" (perhaps by their father). It has also been suggested that sexual contact occurred between the children and their nurse.[8]

In this respect, the Wolf Man was typical. Many of Freud's patients experienced "sexual seduction" as children (this is Freud's term for sexual abuse). In the course of their treatment, many of his female patients told him that they when they were

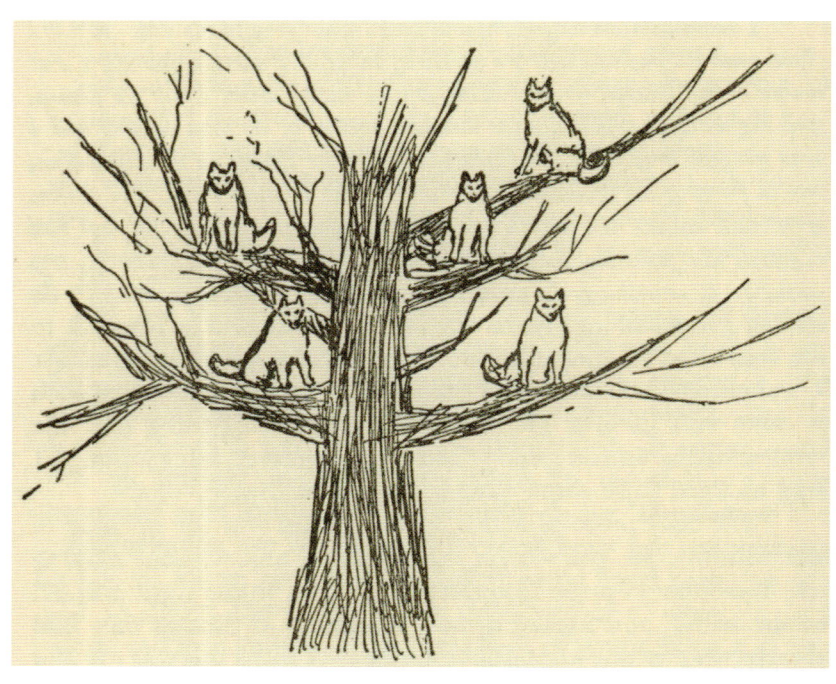

Sergei Pankejeff, Drawing of wolves sitting in a tree, from Sigmund Freud, "From the History of an Infantile Neurosis" (1918), *The Standard Edition of the Complete Psychological Works of Sigmund Freud*, vol. 17 (1917–1919), ed. James Strachey (London: Hogarth Press, 1955).

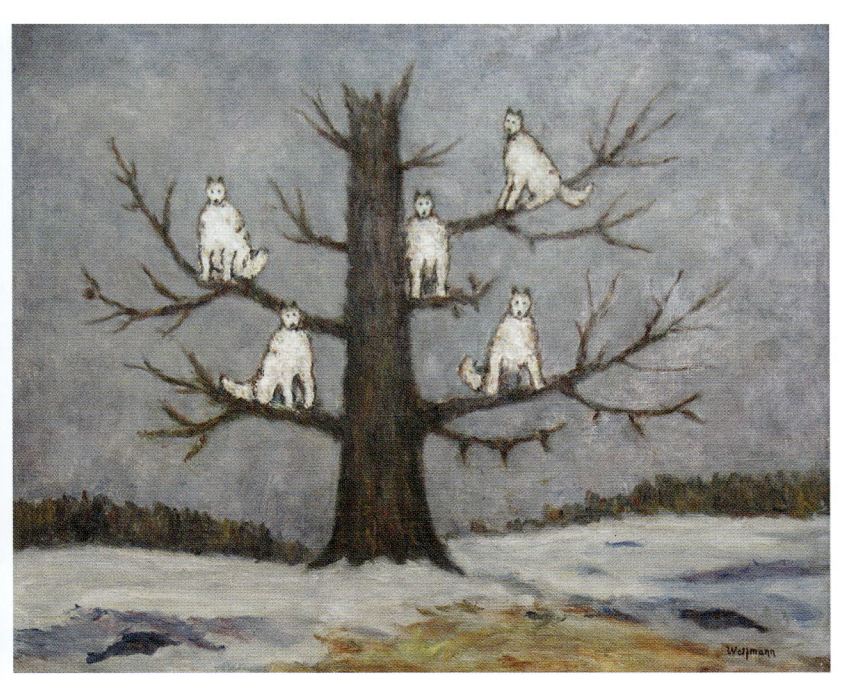

Sergei Pankejeff, Painting of wolves sitting in a tree, 1965, oil
on board. Courtesy of the Freud Museum London.

children, they were sexually abused by men (servants, teachers, family friends, and sometimes family members). And many of his male patients, like Sergei, were abused by nursemaids or governesses. On the occasions where there was evidence of "precocious" sexual activity between siblings, Freud often found that one sibling was simply repeating activities that they themselves had been subject to in a prior assault.

Freud made a radical leap to suggest that these childhood abuses were traumatic in nature and formative to his patients' subsequent suffering as adults. In a few instances, he chastised his professional colleagues for not doing enough to safeguard childhood sexually. The medical community responded to his claims with a resounding silence. It took several more decades for the establishment to begin to acknowledge the extent of this violence.

When Sergei's sister was twenty, she traveled to the Caucasus, overdosed on a poisonous substance, and died. At this point, Sergei fell into his first significant depression. He attended university as was planned, but a few years later, in 1908, Pankejeff's father also died suddenly, leaving the young man heir to the vast family fortune. A debilitating depression immediately overtook him. After several unsuccessful treatments in a variety of hospitals across Europe, Sergei traveled to Vienna to begin an analysis with Freud. The treatment lasted four years. After a short period of respite from his illness, Pankejeff returned to Vienna, having been stripped of his immense wealth by the Russian Revolution.

Freud presents a long and complicated analysis but, in short, suggests that behind his patient's dream of the wolves lay another important, albeit forgotten, memory, which he called "the primal scene." This is a scene the dreamer has witnessed but has been subsequently repressed. Freud reconstructs the primal scene from analytic evidence provided by his patient: baby Sergei must have witnessed his parents having sexual intercourse while he lay in his crib nearby. It was only later that this infantile memory became significant, Freud suggests,

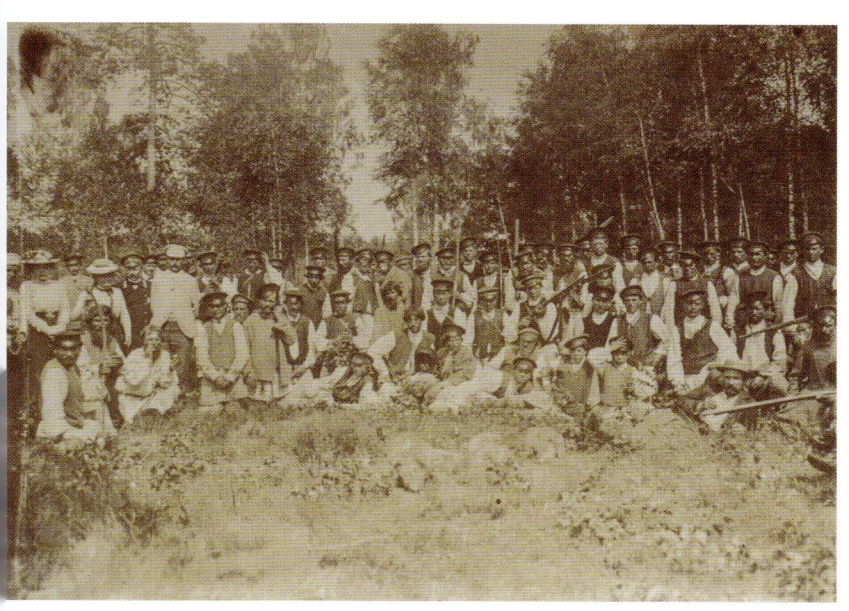

Unknown photographer, A wolf hunt on the Pankejeff estate in
White Russia, before 1905. Anna, Sergei, and their mother
are seated center right. Reproduced from the Pankejeff Collections
of the Library of Congress.

W IS FOR WHITE WOLVES

after Sergei's childhood sexuality was awakened by his sister's "seduction."

The path that Freud takes to connect a child's nightmare about wolves to an earlier scene in which the child witnessed his parents having sex is far from clear (the doctor provides an exhaustive explanation in a footnote).[9] But this case paved a new understanding of the deferred nature of trauma—how the memory and force of a childhood experience can return later in life and how the impact of sexual violence unfolds.

As the contemporary psychologist Gabor Maté has put it: "trauma is not the bad things that happen to us, but rather what happens *inside* of us because of these happenings."[10] We now know that this violence can divide families and communities and stretch across generations. We also know, in part thanks to Freud, that this kind of sexual violence is often psychologically repressed, making the memories difficult to recover and even more difficult to bring to speech. Thankfully, we have another way to see this trauma.

For all the criticism leveled against Freud for his extravagant interpretations of the Wolf Man's case, what remains crucial is his focus on the importance of Pankejeff's nightmare. The dream became a key to understanding the force of childhood trauma and the way these experiences are relived.[11] The precision of the language here is important. Freud's point was that this kind of sexual violence is not just remembered in the usual sense of the term but is actually *brought back to life*, in part through imaginary scenes that enter the mind unbidden. Pankejeff's nightmare comes to stand in for this other scene of the "seduction." Whatever the details of the seduction might have been, the nightmare serves as the mind's way of both representing the significance of this experience and shielding the dreamer from it.

The French psychoanalyst Didier Anzieu referred to this as the "skin" or "film" of the dream (*pellicule*, in French), a word that captures this dual function: on one hand, dreams work analogously to the fine membranes that envelop and protect plant and animal organisms, and on the other hand, dreams function in the manner of photographic film, like a strip of celluloid that can record and project visual images. Dreams, in Anzieu's terms, repair our psychic skin, mending the attacks on our being that we face from day to day.[12] Dreams represent our primal scenes and serve as our primary defense, providing a protective shield for the mind.

Sergei Pankejeff's life was marked by a series of devastated social bonds, seismic upheavals that were at once intimate, historical, and political. He spent a lifetime trying to tie together the traumas of his individual history and those of history writ large. His childhood dream—and all the voluminous elaborations that it provoked—offers a link to these wounds, and indeed, helped knit them together. Sometimes it is up to dreams to repair our histories.

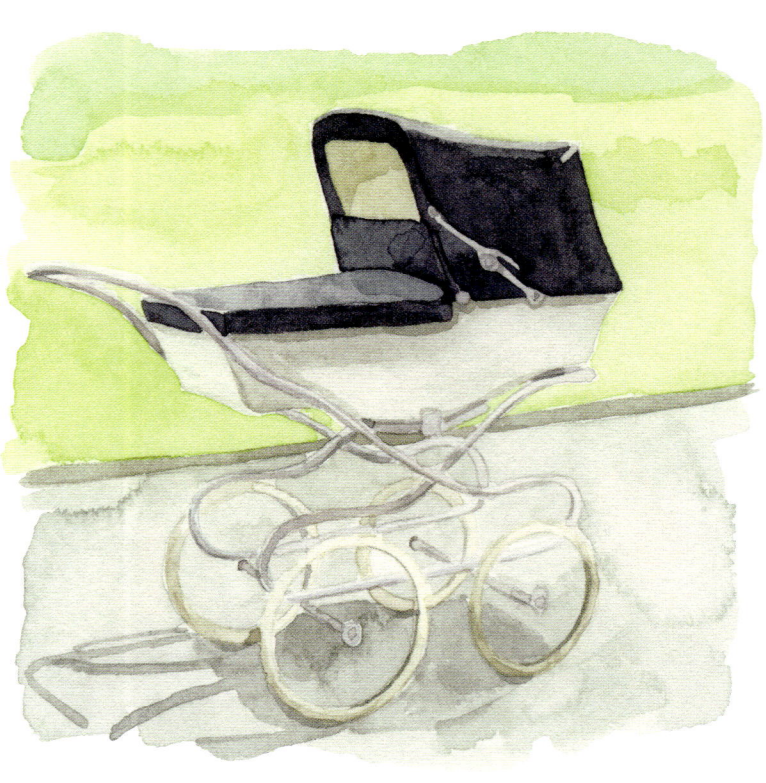

X IS FOR XANAX

Few of the Londoners who we interviewed during the COVID-19 pandemic spoke directly about contracting the virus. Among those who did was Shelley, a woman in her late fifties who has lived in London her whole life. Shelley contracted this disease at the end of March 2020 during the initial stages of the pandemic. Because testing was still months away, she was never officially diagnosed, but she displayed the classic symptoms, including fever, severe respiratory difficulties, and a prolonged loss of her sense of smell.

Like many people who experienced the virus directly, Shelley also had vivid dreams while she was ill, which she described as "like being on an acid trip." Subsequent studies have shown that people who experienced more acute forms of the illness reported more frequent nightmares. Some of the most harrowing accounts come from patients who ended up in intensive care units on respirators.[1]

Shelley had one dream that she was keen to share with us. The vision came to her just after the acute phase of her illness, while she was still recovering:

> I had a dream that I was observing my mother. She was in a supermarket. At the front of the supermarket was a coffee bar. My mum looked young, and she was with my aunt, who also looked young. My mum and my aunt are both still alive. My mum is eighty, my aunt's ninety, but they looked young [in the dream]. I was sitting up high and looking over something: a silver metal bar that was in front of me.[2]

This was the entirety of the dream. Shelley saw her mother and aunt, who appeared to be young. She was sitting up high, and a silver bar obstructed her view. Despite its seeming simplicity, the dream was so vivid that as soon as she woke up, she felt a strong need to contact her mother.

To her surprise, Shelley's mother confirmed that a supermarket in Finchley, where the family used to live in North London, had a coffee bar in the front. Her mother also confirmed that she and her sister used to visit the supermarket, often leaving Shelley outside in her pram: "In those days—in 1962, I think this would have been—you could leave babies in prams outside the supermarket." And her mother also confirmed one last detail from the dream: Shelley's pram had silver handlebars.

Shelley felt that her dream was significant and recognized the demand to pay attention to it. She also recognized that she needed help in deciphering its significance and the dream told her exactly where to find that help:

> I can't even remember the last time I thought about that place. It doesn't exist anymore. And I never even knew that my pram had silver handlebars, but the dream must have jogged something in the depths of my memory. My aunt and my mom were so delighted that I remembered. Even now, I can see the images flashing past as if in a film. I've got very good memory, but I would never have remembered that. It really hit me that somewhere, in the depths of my memory, there are things that I don't even know that I know.

Being severely ill brought Shelley "back to the beginning," as she put it. She was in bed for nearly six weeks and spent much of that time thinking about her childhood—things she "hadn't really thought about for years."

Two things stand out as significant about Shelley's account. First, being severely ill called forth a vivid dream that returned her to memories of early childhood, particularly her attachment to her primary caregivers. And second, these early memories seemed to exist independently of consciousness: they were beyond the ego's grasp. The dream showed her things that she did not know she knew but that nevertheless felt significant in a time of severe illness.

Vivid dreams, nightmares, and hallucinations are common in the critically ill. So-called fever dreams have been recorded throughout human history (the list includes the infamous dreams that Descartes experienced in November 1619, which biographers suggest were induced when he shut himself in a room with a large fireplace). Recent studies have provided a scientific explanation for what has long been known but has been forgotten in the Western world: *dreams are medicine*.[3]

In neurological terms, dreams correspond to an activation of the emotional and reward systems of the brain. Psychologists have proposed that increased activity in the amygdala and the mesolimbic dopamine system during periods of dream sleep promotes the consolidation of memory traces that have high emotional and motivational value. Activity in the dopamine-releasing region of the brain can create feelings of intense pleasure. Dreaming also appears to benefit other high-level cognitive functions (such as emotional regulation, social cognition, and creativity) because these experiences provide a safe virtual environment in which the dreamer can be exposed to a significant load of rewarding (or aversive) stimuli.[4]

To translate into lay terms: dreaming can sooth the mind and body by releasing a rush of chemical messengers that induce good feelings (in the case of positive dreams), or it can build our cognitive and emotional resilience by forcing us to face a difficult situation, albeit virtually (in the case of bad dreams or nightmares). Again: *dreams are medicine*.

Perhaps not surprisingly, some of these neurological effects can be reproduced by pharmaceuticals. Opioids (with trade names such as OxyContin, Percocet, and Vicodin) and benzodiazepines (such as Ativan, Valium, and Xanax) slow down the central nervous system, causing sedation and muscle relaxation. This can, for a time, lower anxiety levels (specifically, by impacting gamma aminobutyric acid, the chemical responsible for reducing activity in parts of the brain connected to emotion, memory, breathing, and reasoning). These drugs also induce the brain to release dopamine, and taking them can produce deeply pleasurable feelings—at least temporarily.

Each time the drug is taken, however, a higher amount of dopamine is released, which produces a more pleasurable high. This makes these drugs highly addictive, and with prolonged use, they can change the anatomy of the brain, adversely affecting cognitive function, physical, and mental health. Ivan Illich might have categorized these pharmaceuticals as iatrogenetic medicine: with their plethora of side-effects, the drugs are more pathogen than cure.[5]

While these pharmaceuticals can be useful tools that help some people manage a variety of health issues, they cannot address *who a person is* or the complexity of their life world. Xanax can temporarily soothe certain emotional disorders by enhancing the activity of certain neurotransmitters in the brain, but this is a pharmacological substitute for a more holistic psychological, neurobiological, emotional, social, and spiritual process that we call dreaming. Dreams soothe the body by activating the dopamine system, but more importantly, they help ground dreamers in their lifeworld.

There is much to be learned, in this respect, from critical healers and medical practitioners who use dreams as a tool for healing. Among others, this includes the psychiatrist, Eduardo Duran, who for most of his career has worked with Indigenous populations in the United States. Trained in the Western medical tradition, Duran quickly learned the limits of his education once he began working with people in communities that were profoundly affected by the violent processes of colonization. The trauma-informed approach that he developed (with the help of many elders and critical practitioners) is attentive to the larger lifeworlds of his patients. In Duran's view, this intervention represents a return to an older definition of *psyche*: "psychology literally means the study of the soul. Somehow this truth eludes many who work in the world and identify themselves as psychologists."[6] In this approach, dreams provide a crucial portal to the existential dimension of suffering: these visions can lead the dreamer to an understanding of who they are in the greater context of their lifeworld.

These insights from liberation psychology have universal implications. Consider Shelley's case again. The woman's dream brought healing in a time of illness because this psychological event had physiological effects, soothing the body and mind through the activation of the dopamine system. More important, though, the dream placed her back in the time and place of her early childhood. At a time when Shelley found herself critically ill, her dream life renewed and reinforced a primary attachment. Ailing and bedridden, the dream returned the dreamer to her mother's care.

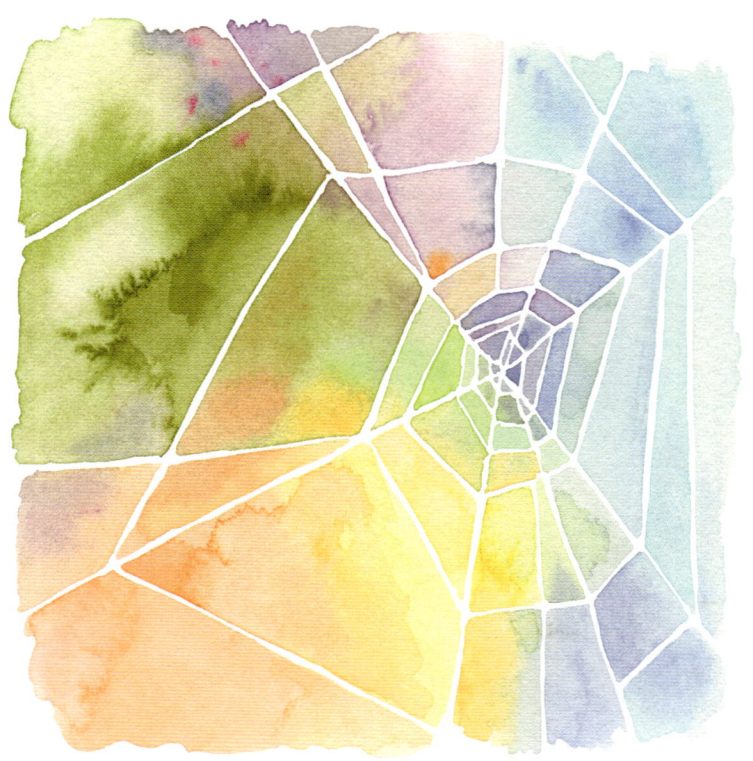

Y IS FOR YOU

One of the best pieces of advice that the ancient dream interpreter Artemidorus offered to his readers was to "patiently listen" to the dreams of others.[1] I hope this book has provided opportunities to exercise this advice. Listening to people speak about their dreams has been a deeply transformative practice for me. I hope this book has convinced you to try this special form of listening for yourself.

This chapter is a bit more practical in nature. It is my attempt to put into words some of the lessons I have learned about how to work directly with your own dreams. Nurturing a relationship with your dreams takes a measure of practice and intentionality. For people who struggle to remember these visions, often a little autosuggestion will help. As you turn out the light at night, tell yourself that you will remember your dreams. Use a convincing tone. And as soon as you wake in the morning, give yourself a few quiet moments to let the dream images swim back to you. Sometimes it helps to write them down. But I strongly advise you to avoid looking at your phone first thing in the morning. Hold off the impositions of reality for as long as you can. Give yourself time with your dreams. Along these lines, I have three more concrete pieces of advice:

1. *Respect the value of sleep*. One of the most important ways to attend to your dream life is to properly prepare yourself for sleep. This does not involve buying anything. Sleep has become an arena of economic exploitation full of specialized mattresses, luxury bedding, sleep trackers, and supplements. As the self-proclaimed Nap Bishop, Tricia Hersey, teaches us, capitalism has territorialized this landscape to the point that even rest has come to be defined in terms of productivity.[2] Sleep is not just the time needed to recharge our batteries for the next day's work.

This is a spectacular degradation of a landscape that for thousands of years was understood to be the ultimate plane for healing and regeneration. Unsurprisingly, contemporary liberation movements have seized upon rest and sleep as the grounds of political resistance—a way to reclaim human dignity from the oppressiveness of grind culture.

Respecting the value of sleep also means recognizing that you must *surrender* to this experience. Dreaming is not something that can be consciously willed. This mode of seeing cannot be accessed through reason or rational investigation. Dreams do not speak to the cogito. In a certain sense, these visions disable our conscious relationship to knowledge (including self-knowledge). As the existential psychologist, Ludwig Binswanger, once put it, "To dream means: I don't know what is happening to me."[3] Paradoxically, undergoing this trial of not knowing what is happening grants dreamers access to another form of nonrational knowledge. And access is granted precisely because the dreamers are *not* the master of their dreams. Embrace this state of *not* knowing.

2. *Follow the associations.* Dreams show rather than tell. And part of what they manifest is our unique bond to the social imaginary. These visions locate us within the matrix of our social environments, revealing the ways we are tethered or, as the case may be, fixed within our milieu.

Certain psychosocial techniques can be useful for grasping and working with this revelatory aspect of dream life. These techniques extend the logic of the dreaming process, helping us to assimilate the nonrational knowledge that is being offered and thereby enhancing the dream's organic capacity for transformation.

This approach shifts attention from the dream as a whole to focus the dream's individual parts. Try working with each element of the dream in turn. What associations come to mind when you turn your mental eye to each of these elements? Following our associations and letting the mind move freely from one thought to another—quieting the cogito's demand to "make sense"—can allow unexpected connections to our waking life to emerge. Associative thinking is a particularly creative form of thought that allows us to make unexpected links between seemingly disparate ideas. As Sigmund Freud once said, following these links allows the dreamer to discover "the bridge from the apparently remote dream-world to real life."[4]

Sometimes our associations come in a flood, and sometimes they refuse to come at all, and the mind goes blank. It can be difficult to get in touch with this mode of thinking. It took me several years to learn to associate freely because it required letting go of the rational forms of thinking in which I had been trained. For a long time, I refused to believe that thoughts that just "come to mind" held any value. If this sounds like you, don't give up. As with most things, we get better with practice. The imagination is an organ that grows with use.

Often our associations will lead us to ideas or events from the days immediately preceding the dream. But you may also find yourself recalling memories from long ago. Sometimes the connections seem obvious, but sometimes the thoughts that enter our minds seem completely unrelated to the dream. Trust that all associations are important.

Following these associative chains of thought is a highly effective method for discovering what Ella Freeman Sharpe called "the revelation of the unknown, implicit in the known."[5] In a therapeutic context, this technique has been shown to lead to significant emotional growth and a deepened sense of aliveness. But beyond this context, attending to dream life can radically expand our awareness of the world and generate new ways of seeing and new modes of relating.

3. *Share your dreams.* A dream can be a powerful experience, but the gesture of sharing these visions allows this way of seeing to become a social force. Sharing a dream is one of the most radical forms of communication we possess. It connects us with the transcendental plane, and its spontaneous nature allows us

to find words that matter, transforming a private experience into a potent medium for remaking the world.

Perhaps the best-known example of this gesture is the speech that Martin Luther King Jr. delivered in August 1963 at the steps of the Lincoln Memorial during the March on Washington for Jobs and Freedom. According to his speech writer, Clarence B. Jones, the content of King's now famous address was debated late into the night. Final copies were rushed to the press on the morning of the speech. And when King stepped up to the podium that day, he stuck to the script for about twelve minutes.

But then something extraordinary happened. During one of his pauses, King's close confidant, the gospel singer Mahalia Jackson, shouted words of encouragement: "Tell 'em about the dream, Martin!" The call demanded a response. King pushed the script to one side and gave himself over to the moment. Almost the entire second half of this famous speech is improvised.[6] In film footage from that day, King never returns to his notes. And if I asked you what you recall from this address, I suspect what would come to mind is that irresistibly arresting repeating riff: "*I have a dream*." This dream is often remembered as a vision of a multiracial liberal democracy. The part of King's dream that is less well remembered is his vision of economic redistribution and the end of US imperialism.

This is a famous example, but perhaps a more instructive one comes from one of MLK's teachers, Ella Baker, whose similar entreaty is less often quoted: "This may only be a dream of mine, but I think it can be made real."[7] Baker's behind-the-scenes career as an activist in some of the most influential organizations of the civil rights movement spanned five decades. Among other things, she is remembered for cofounding the Student Nonviolent Coordinating Committee in 1960 and for helping to organize the 1961 Freedom Rides. She was critical of charismatic leaders (she frequently insisted that the "movement made King" and not the other way around). She advocated for grassroots organizing and for what she described as radical democracy:

"my theory is, strong people don't need strong leaders." Baker believed that the most powerful social transformation would come from "ordinary people" who learned to "understand their position and understand their potential power and how to use it."[8] This quietly radical approach guides much of my thinking in this book.

It is hard to overstate the importance of the relatively simple gesture of giving voice to these seemingly private experiences. By sharing our dreams, we testify to our lived experience and affirm who we are by situating ourselves in relationship to our listeners and to the transcendental world of the dream. This disclosure allows us to weave ourselves into the fabric of humanity anew. In this way, attending to dream life is transformative for the self, but it is also transformative for the shared world that lies between us. The act of disclosing these visions has potential to change every constellation.

My phrasing may sound somewhat grand, but my hope is that each of these chapters has provided evidence for the ways that sharing these visions can restructure our relationships to ourselves and others, shift our ways being, and perhaps most importantly, bring new worlds into view—worlds that we have yet to collectively imagine. Dreams can teach us so much about the transformative power of the imagination and the ways we can reenvision the world—*with eyes closed*.

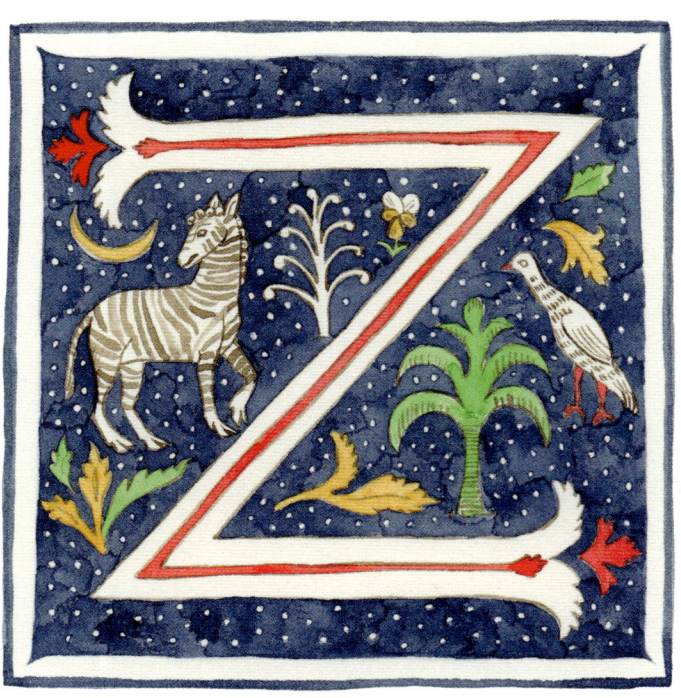

Z IS FOR ZED

Among his private notes, the Roman emperor, Marcus Aurelius, recorded this startling line: "treat everything around you as a dream."[1] Contemporary readers can glean what he might have meant from another note recorded a few pages earlier: "Like seeing roasted meat and other dishes in front of you and suddenly realizing: This is dead fish. A dead bird. A dead pig. Or that this noble vintage is grape juice, and the purple robes are sheep wool dyed with shellfish blood."[2] Our habitual ways of seeing are clouded with layers of invented meanings. Marcus counsels us to see through these "perceptions," to pierce them, so we can see what things "really are." Dreams entreat us to question how we see the world, the emperor seems to say. These visions demand we strip away the "legends that encrust" our waking sight. The note is a kind of practical reminder to himself to develop a disciplined way of seeing so that he can form a proper relationship to the world.

Meditations is full of this kind of practical advice. Surprisingly, the book was never meant to be published. In fact, Marcus had no expectation that anyone else would read it, which makes the advice feel even more poignant.

The book opens with a series of reflections on what the emperor has learned from his family and ancestors, his teachers and fellow philosophers. The list includes the qualities Marcus admires in others and well as a lengthy acknowledgment of his debt to divine providence. Taken together, this section of the book reads as an expression of profound humility—an extended acknowledgement of all that he owes to others.

In the same spirt, here is my (partial) list of the debts and lessons I accrued while writing this book:

1.

Melinda: An eye that delights in detail. One of the best teachers of the ways that images can be transformed into words and back into images again. These gorgeous illustrations.

2.

Martina: What it means to bear witness. A special capacity to see but also to listen to others and to the self. That time you listened to your intuition and came back to find me in Edinburgh made everything possible. So much joy in genuine collaboration.

3.

Noel: Quality of attention + curiosity = the best recipe for intelligence. An ability to respond to others' suffering with courage and delicacy. A rare capacity to meet life's blows with grace and humility. Brotherly love.

4.

Yigal: Hospitality—how to use food to bring people together in communion. How to care. An irrepressible curiosity and surrealist pleasure in the materiality of life. Sartorial style. Also, brotherly love.

5.

Deborah, Alice, David: What it means to teach—to be guided by generosity and hope, always, even in the face of breakdown. Especially in the face of breakdown.

6.

To be blessed in friendship makes a commitment to life possible: Chris, Danielle, Emma, Gabby, Jeremy, Juanita, Lily, Matthew, Nassim, Nataleah, Norma, Raimondo, Sasha, and Susan. Our lively conversations have sustained me over these years.

7.

Creative collaborations that open doorways in the mind and in reality: Foteini Aravani (Museum of London), Amber Jacobs (Birkbeck, University of London), Ruth Noack (Dutch Art

Institute and The Corner at Whitman-Walker), Fabrice Roman (La Roseraie), Bodhan Shumylovych and colleagues (Center for Urban History of East Central Europe), and Christiane Solte-Gresser and Patricia Oster-Stierle (Saarland University).

8.

The team at the MIT Press for shepherding this book into the world: Victoria Hindley, Gabriela Bueno Gibbs, Deborah Cantor-Adams, Margarita Encomienda, as well as my copyeditor, Rosemary Winfield. I am grateful for the generous financial support provided by the Social Sciences and Humanities Research Council of Canada and Western University.

9.

The guardians of sleep: all the Londoners who shared their dreams during the COVID-19 pandemic, all the volunteers who helped collect them, and the talented Andrew Braun and Erin McIndoe Sproule who helped provide a beautiful backdrop for listening. A model for how a creative partnership can make something greater than the sum of its parts. This project offered so many remarkable and unexpected lessons in generosity, hospitality, listening, attention, relationality, and connection.

10.

This book exists because of the Black and Indigenous traditions that have, against considerable pressure, protected and cherished the transcendental knowledge offered in dream life. So many activists, scholars, artists, and practitioners have provided teachings about how to attend to this domain: Octavia Butler, Eduardo Duran, Abigail Echo-Hawk, Frantz Fanon, Margaret Kovach, Amy Shawanda, Leanne Betasamosake Simpson, Lewis Williams, among many others.

11.

There is nothing that is at once so ordinary and so extraordinary as the work of mourning. Those recently and not so recently departed—Carol, Eugenia, Dad—you are on every page. I cherish your visits in my dreams.

12.

Sofia: Wisdom (of course). The capacity to always be right and to always aim for the truth. How to love. A practical imagination that finds ways to improve the lives of the people around you. Patience and optimism in the face of disappointments and accidents. The capacity to cause a deep and previously unknown happiness. This book is for you—because of you—even as its flaws remain my own.

ILLUSTRATIONS BY MELINDA JOSIE

Attention, 2024
Boa Constrictor, 2024
Cancer, 2024
Defense, 2024
Evil, 2024
Filing Cabinet, 2024
Grief, 2024
Homework, 2024
Intergenerational, 2024
Jealousy, 2024
Kids, 2024
Liberation, 2024
Monster, 2024
Nightmare, 2024
Otoscope, 2024
Princess, 2024
Quackery, 2024
Refuge, 2024
Suicide, 2024
Trans, 2024
Utopia, 2024
Vegetables, 2024
White Wolves, 2024
Xanax, 2024
You, 2024
Zed, 2024

NOTES

INTRODUCTION

1   John Berger, "Uses of Photography" (1978), in *About Looking* (New York: Vintage, 1999), 55.

2   Frantz Fanon, *Black Skin, White Masks* (1952), trans. Charles Lam Markmann (New York: Grove Press, 1967), 104.

3   Fanon, *Black Skin, White Masks*, 105. I am indebted to Sylvia Wynter's reading of Fanon's notion of the socius in "Towards the Sociogenic Principle: Fanon, Identity, the Puzzle of Conscious Experience, and What It Is Like to Be 'Black,'" in *National Identities and Socio-Political Changes in Latin America*, ed. Antonio Gomez-Moriana and Mercedes Duran-Cogan (New York: Routledge, 2013), 30–66. For a good overview of clinical theory on dreams since Freud's time, see Sara Flanders, ed., *The Dream Discourses Today* (London: Routledge, 1993).

4   I borrow this idea from anthropologist Michael Jackson, *The Politics of Storytelling: Variations on a Theme by Hannah Arendt*, 2nd ed. (Copenhagen: Museum Musculanum Press, 2002), 37.

5   Fanon, *Black Skin, White Masks*, 229.

6   Stephen Gaukroger, *Descartes: An Intellectual Biography* (Oxford: Clarendon Press, 1995), 106–109.

7   For a more fulsome account of Descartes's dreams, see Gaukroger, *Descartes*, 106–109.

8   René Descartes, *Meditations on First Philosophy* (1641), ed. and trans. John Cottingham, (Cambridge: Cambridge University Press, 2013), 37.

9   Barbara Tedlock identified Cartesian dualism as the source of the devaluation of dream life in *Dreaming: Anthropological and Psychological Interpretations* (Santa Fe, NM: School of American Research Press, 1992). See also Edward McGushin, "The Role of Descartes's Dream in the Meditations and the Historical Ontology of Ourselves," *Foucault Studies* 25 (2018): 84–102. For an overview of the scientific resistance to the study of dreaming, see Robert Haskell, "Cognitive Psychology and Dream Research: Historical, Conceptual, and Epistemological Considerations," *Journal of Mind and Behavior* 7, no. 2/3 (1986): 131–159.

10   Aníbal Quijano, "Coloniality of Power, Eurocentrism, and Latin America," *International Sociology* 15, no. 2 (2000): 215–232.

11   Sigmund Freud, "Introductory Lectures on Psycho-analysis" (1917), in *The Standard Edition of the Complete Psychological Works of Sigmund Freud*, vol. 16, ed. James Strachey (London: Hogarth Press, 1955), 285.

12   Leanne Betasamosake Simpson, *Dancing on Turtle's Back: Stories of Nishnaabeg Re-Creation Resurgence, and a New Emergence* (Winnipeg, Manitoba: Arbeiter Ring Publishing, 2011), 44.

13   Tore Nielsen, "Infectious Dreams," *Scientific American*, October 1, 2020, https://www.scientificamerican.com/article/the-covid-19-pandemic-is-changing-our-dreams/.

14   Giuseppe Civitarese, "Heart of Darkness in the Courtyard, or Dreaming the COVID-19 Pandemic," *American Psychoanalytic Association* 38, no. 2 (2021): 133–135.

15   Sylvia Wynter, "Unsettling the Coloniality of Being/Power/Truth/Freedom: Towards the Human, after Man, Its Overrepresentation—An Argument," *CR: The New Centennial Review* 3, no. 3 (Fall 2003): 257–337.

16   I owe this insight to Noga Rotem, who offered this direction in her review of my earlier book, *Dreaming in Dark Times* (Minneapolis: Minnesota University Press, 2017). Noga Rotem, "Book Review of 'Dreaming in Dark Times' by Sharon Sliwinski," *International Journal of Dream Research* 12, no. 1 (2019): 160–162.

A IS FOR ATTENTION

1   Francis Crick and Graeme Mitchison, "The Function of Dream Sleep," *Nature* 304, no. 5922 (1983): 111–114.

2   The neuroscience of dreaming has grown quickly. Among other works, see Mark Solms, *The Feeling Brain: Selected Papers on Psychoanalysis* (New York: Routledge, 2018); Mark Solms, *The Neuropsychology of Dreams: A Clinical-anatomical Study* (New York: Psychology Press, 1997); Antonio Zadra and Robert Stickgold, *When Brains Dream: Understanding the Science and Mystery of Our Dreaming Minds* (New York: Norton, 2022).

3   Sidarta Ribeiro, *The Oracle of the Night: The History and Science of Dream*, trans. Daniel Hahn (New York: Pantheon, 2021).

4   Sigmund Freud, *The Interpretation of Dreams* (1900), in *The Standard Edition of the Complete Psychological Works of Sigmund Freud*, vol. 5, ed. James Strachey (London: Hogarth Press, 1953), 506 n. 2. Freud repeats this idea in "Remarks on the Theory and Practice of Dream-Interpretation" (1923), in *Standard Edition*, vol. 19, 112; in "History of the Psychoanalytic Movement" (1914), in *Standard Edition*, vol. 14, 65; and in "Some Neurotic Mechanisms" (1922), in *Standard Edition*, vol. 17, 229.

5   Sigmund Freud, "Recommendations to Physicians Practicing Psycho-analysis" (1912), in *Standard Edition*, vol. 12, 111.

6   Freud, "Recommendations to Physicians Practicing Psycho-analysis," 112.

7   Freud, "Recommendations to Physicians Practicing Psychoanalysis," 112.

8   For an extended discussion of Freud's term, see Giuseppe Civitarese, "On Bion's Concepts of Negative Capability and Faith," *Psychoanalytic Quarterly* 88, no. 4 (2019): 751–783; Theodor Reik, *Listening with the Third Ear* (New York: Farrar, Strauss, and Giroux, 1949).

9   Dylan Robinson, *Hungry Listening: Resonant Theory for Indigenous Sound Studies* (Minneapolis: University of Minnesota Press, 2020), 37.

10   See Tressie McMillan Cottom, "The Dolly Moment: Why We Stan a Post-Racism Queen," Substack, February 25, 2021, https://tressie .substack.com/p/the-dolly-moment, and "The Enduring, Invisible Power of Blonde," *New York Times*, January 19, 2023, https://www.nytimes .com/2023/01/19/opinion/the-enduring-invisible-power-of-blond.html.

11   Richard Dyer, "The Matter of Whiteness," in *White Privilege: Essential Readings on the Other Side of Racism*, 2nd ed., ed. Paula Rothenberg (New York: Worth, 2011), 10.

12   Nicholas Mirzoeff, *White Sight: Visual Politics and Practices of Whiteness* (Cambridge, MA: MIT Press, 2023).

B IS FOR BOA CONSTRICTOR

1   Mary Shelley, "Introduction" (1831), *Frankenstein; or, The Modern Prometheus* (1818), ed. D. L. MacDonald and Kathleen Scherf (Peterborough, Ontario: Broadview Press, 1999), 356.

2   Friedrich Schelling, *System of Transcendental Idealism* (1800), cited and discussed at length in Richard Kearney's sprawling study, *The Wake of Imagination: Toward Postmodern Culture* (New York: Routledge, 1988), 180.

C IS FOR CANCER

1   Audre Lorde, *The Cancer Journals* (1980) (New York: Penguin, 2020), 48

2   Lorde, *The Cancer Journals*, 48.

3   Lorde, *The Cancer Journals*, 44.

4   Audre Lorde, "Notes from a Trip to Russia" (1977), in *Sister Outsider: Essays and Speeches* (Berkeley: Crossing Press, 2007), 13–35.

5   Audre Lorde, "Poetry Is Not a Luxury" (1977), in *Sister Outsider: Essays and Speeches*, 37–38.

D IS FOR DEFENSE

1   Mandela claims he uttered these words during a meeting he called with various local and foreign reporters after the three-day workers' strike was crushed in May 1961. See Nelson Mandela, *Long Walk to*

Freedom (Boston: Little, Brown, 1994), 270. He said something similar during his first televised interview, which he gave to the British television network ITN around the same time. Available online at Alexis C. Madrigal, "Nelson Mandela's First TV Interview, May 1961," *The Atlantic*, December 6, 2013, www.theatlantic.com/international /archive/2013/12/nelson-mandelas-first-tv-interview-may-1961/282120.

2   Mandela, *Long Walk to Freedom*, 390.

3   Mandela, *Long Walk to Freedom*, 496.

4   Excerpts of Mandela's speech are reprinted in his autobiography, and an audio recording is available at Alex Purcell, Richard Sprenger, and Mustafa Khalili, "Nelson Mandela, 1964: 'I Am Prepared to Die'— Audio Recording of Speech at Sabotage Trial," *The Guardian*, December 5, 2013, http://www.theguardian.com/world/video/2013/dec/05/nelson -mandela-1964-speech-audio.

5   Mandela, *Long Walk to Freedom*, 570.

6   Reading them psychoanalytically, negative statements are generally understood as taking note of what is repressed. In his paper "Negation," Freud writes, "With the help of the symbol of negation, thinking frees itself from the restrictions of repression." Sigmund Freud, "Negation" (1925), in *The Standard Edition of the Complete Psychological Works of Sigmund Freud*, vol. 19, ed. James Strachey (London: Hogarth Press, 1961), 239.

7   *Mandela: Long Walk to Freedom*, directed by Justin Chadwick (Pathé, 2013).

8   Robert L. Miller, "From the Publisher," *Time*, February 5, 1990, 10.

9   Mandela, *Long Walk to Freedom*, 144.

10   Didier Anzieu, *The Skin Ego: A Psychoanalytic Approach to Self* (1985), trans. Naomi Segal (London: Routledge, 2018), 238.

11   This is a shortened and revised version of a chapter that appears in Sharon Sliwinski, *Dreaming in Dark Times: Six Exercises in Political Thought* (Minneapolis: University of Minnesota Press, 2017).

E IS FOR EVIL

1   Robert Jay Lifton, *Witness to an Extreme Century* (New York: Free Press, 2011), 239.

2   Robert Jay Lifton, *The Nazi Doctors: Medical Killing and the Psychology of Genocide* (New York: Basic Books, 1986), 15.

3   Christian Pross, "Breaking through the Postwar Coverup of Nazi Doctors in Germany," *Journal of Medical Ethics* 17 (1991): 13–16.

4   Lifton, *The Nazi Doctors*, 103.

5   Lifton, *The Nazi Doctors*, 105.

F IS FOR FILING CABINET

1   Except where otherwise identified, all quotations are from Sofia Locklear's interview with Abigail Echo-Hawk in Detroit on October 6, 2022. The full interview can be heard at Sharon Sliwinski, host, *Guardians of Sleep*, season 2, episode 1, "Abigail Echo-Hawk," The Museum of Dreams, November 15, 2024, https://www.museumof dreams.org/guardians-of-sleep/2024/11/15/episode-7-abigail-echo -hawk-1. Used with permission.

2   Abigail Echo-Hawk, "Our Bodies Our Stories: Sexual Violence Among Native Women in Seattle, WA," Urban Indian Health Initiative, published August 23, 2022, https://www.uihi.org/resources /our-bodies-our-stories.

3   Annita Lucchesi and Abigail Echo-Hawk, "Missing and Murdered Indigenous Women and Girls: A Snapshot of Data from 71 Urban Cities in the United States," Urban Indian Health Initiative, created November 14, 2018, last updated April 25, 2022, https://www.uihi.org/download /missing-and-murdered-indigenous-women-girls.

4   See Danielle Taschereau Mamers, *Settler Colonial Ways of Seeing: Documentation, Administration, and the Interventions of Indigenous Art* (Minneapolis: University of Minnesota Press, 2023).

G IS FOR GRIEF

1   Sophus Helle, *Gilgamesh: A New Translation of the Ancient Epic* (New Haven, CT: Yale University Press, 2021), 4.

2   Rivkah Harris, "Images of Women in the Gilgamesh Epic," in *Lingering over Words: Studies in Ancient Near Eastern Literature in Honor of William L. Moran*, ed. Tzvi Abusch, John Huehnergard, and Piotr Steinkeller, Harvard Semitic Studies 37 (Leiden: Brill Academic Publishers, 1990), 219–230.

3   Audre Lorde, "The Uses of the Erotic," *The Selected Works of Audre Lorde*, ed. Roxane Gay (New York: Norton, 2020).

4   Helle, *Gilgamesh*, 10

5   Helle, *Gilgamesh*, 12.

6   Helle, *Gilgamesh*, 13.

7   James Baldwin, *Giovanni's Room* (1956) (New York: Knopf, 2024), 57

8   Helle, *Gilgamesh*, 63.

9   Helle, *Gilgamesh*, 72.

10   Helle, *Gilgamesh*, 112.

11   James Baldwin, *Another Country* (1962) (New York: Vintage, 1993), 340.

12   James Baldwin, *The Fire Next Time* (1963), in *The Price of the Ticket: Collected Nonfiction 1948–1985* (New York: St. Martin's Press, 1985), 375.

H IS FOR HOMEWORK

1   Philip Leymarie, "Painful Memories of the Revolt of 1947: Deafening Silence on a Horrifying Repression," *Le Monde Diplomatique*, March 1997, http://mondediplo.com/1997/03/02madagascar. See also J. Tronchon, *L'Insurection Malgache de 1947* (Paris: Maspero, 1974).

2   Jean Fremigacci, "La vérité sur la grande révolte de Madagascar," *L'Histoire* (March 2007): 318, https://www.lhistoire.fr/la-vérité-sur -la-grande-révolte-de-madagascar.

3   Maurice Bloch, "Foreword," in Octave Mannoni, *Prospero and Caliban: The Psychology of Colonization* (1950), 2nd ed., trans. Pamela Powesland (Ann Arbor: University of Michigan Press, 1990), v.

4   Mannoni, *Prospero and Caliban*, 6.

5   Mannoni, *Prospero and Caliban*, 89–93.

6   Mannoni, *Prospero and Caliban*, 89.

7   Frantz Fanon, *Black Skin, White Masks* (1952), trans. Charles Lam Markmann (New York: Grove Press, 1967). For more on Fanon's understanding of dream life see Vicky Lebeau, "Psychopolitics: Frantz Fanon's *Black Skin, White Masks*," in *Psycho-Politics and Cultural Desires*, eds. Jan Campbell and Janet Harbord (London: UCL Press, 1998), 107–117, and David Marriott, "On Racial Fetishism," *Qui Parle* 18, no. 2 (2010): 215–248.

8   Fanon, *Black Skin, White Masks,* 77–78 (emphasis in original).

I IS FOR INTERGENERATIONAL

1   Paul Stamets, *Mycelium Running: How Mushrooms Can Help Save the World* (New York: Ten Speed Press, 2005), 1.

2   Suzanne Simard, *Finding the Mother Tree: Discovering the Wisdom of the Forest* (Toronto: Penguin, 2021), 5 (emphasis in original).

3   Sigmund Freud, *The Interpretation of Dreams*, in *The Standard Edition of the Complete Psychological Works of Sigmund Freud*, vol. 5, ed. James Strachey (London: Hogarth, 1953), 525.

4   Robin Wall Kimmerer, *Braiding Sweetgrass: Indigenous Wisdom, Scientific Knowledge, and the Teaching of Plants* (Minneapolis, MN: Milkweed Editions, 2013), 337.

5   Interview with Lewis Williams conducted November 17, 2022.

6   Lewis Williams, Rose Roberts, and Alastair McIntosh, *Radical Human Ecology: Intercultural and Indigenous Approaches* (New York: Routledge, 2016), 3.

7   Interview with Lewis Williams conducted November 17, 2022.

8 Lewis Williams, "The Human Ecologist as Alchemist: An Inquiry into Ngāi Te Rangi Cosmology, Human Agency, and Well-Being in a Time of Ecological Peril," in *Radical Human Ecology: Intercultural and Indigenous Approaches*, ed. Lewis Williams, Rose Roberts, and Alastair McIntosh (New York: Routledge, 2016), 106.

J IS FOR JEALOUSY

1 Genesis 37:4 (New Revised Standard Version).

2 Genesis 41:16 (New Revised Standard Version).

3 Genesis 41:39 (New Revised Standard Version).

4 Genesis 46:30 (New Revised Standard Version).

5 Juliet Mitchell has written a series of books on siblings, including *Fratriarchy: The Sibling Trauma and the Law of the Mother* (London: Routledge, 2023) and *Siblings: Sex and Violence* (London: Wiley, 2003).

K IS FOR KIDS

1 Interview with Iris and her mother, Pinny, conducted February 2021. All quotations in this chapter come from this interview, excerpts of which can be heard at Sharon Sliwinski, host, *Guardians of Sleep*, season 1, episode 4, "Pinny and Iris," The Museum of Dreams, September 28, 2021, www.museumofdreams.org/guardians-of-sleep/2021/9/28 /episode-4.

2 Hani Morgan, "Alleviating the Challenges with Remote Learning during a Pandemic," *Educational Sciences* 12, no. 2 (2022): 1–12.

3 T. A. Nielsen et al., "Development of Disturbing Dreams during Adolescence and Their Relation to Anxiety Symptoms," *Sleep* 23, no. 6 (September 15, 2000): 727–736.

4 Jean Piaget, *Play, Dreams and Imitation in Childhood* (London: Routledge, 1951), 154.

5 Donald W. Winnicott, "Communication between Infant and Mother, and Mother and Infant, Compared and Contrasted," in *The Collected Works of D. W. Winnicott*, vol. 8, *1967–1968*, ed. Lesley Caldwell and Helen Robinson (Oxford: Oxford University Press, 2017), 231.

L IS FOR LIBERATION

1 John Stauffer, Zoe Trodd, and Celeste-Marie Bernier, *Picturing Frederick Douglass: An Illustrated Biography of the Nineteenth Century's Most Photographed American* (New York: Liveright / Norton, 2015).

2 I am indebted here to Shawn Michelle Smith's reading of Tubman's portrait in Smith, "Photography, Darkness, and the Underground Railroad: Dawoud Bey's *Night Coming Tenderly, Black,*" *American Quarterly,* 73, no. 1 (March 2021): 25-52. See also Chantal

N. Gibson and Monique Silverman, "Sur/rendering Her Image: The Unknowable Harriet Tubman," *RACAR: Canadian Art Review* 30, no. 1/2 (2005): 25–38. For more information about the *carte de visite* and the Howland album, see Allison Keyes, "A Previously Unknown Portrait of a Young Harriet Tubman Goes on View," *Smithsonian Magazine*, March 26, 2019, https://www.smithsonianmag.com/smithsonian-institution/previously-unknown-portrait-abolitionist-harriet-tubman-young-woman-goes-view-180971796.

3   Claudia Rankine and Beth Loffreda, "Introduction," in *The Racial Imaginary: Writers on Race in the Life of the Mind*, ed. Claudia Rankine, Beth Loffreda, and Max King Cap (Albany, NY: Fence Books, 2015), also available online as "On Whiteness and the Racial Imaginary," *Literary Hub*, April 9, 2015, https://lithub.com/on-whiteness-and-the-racial-imaginary.

4   Tina Campt, *A Black Gaze* (Cambridge, MA: MIT Press, 2021), 7.

5   Sarah Hopkins Bradford, *Scenes in the Life of Harriet Tubman* (Auburn, NY: W. J. Moses, 1869), 79.

6   Bradford, *Scenes in the Life of Harriet Tubman*, 56.

7   Saidiya Hartman, "Preface: The Hold of Slavery," in *Scenes of Subjection: Terror, Slavery, and Self-Making in Nineteenth-Century America* (New York: Norton, 2020), xxxii.

8   Benjamin Drew, *A North-side View of Slavery. The Refugee: Or the Narratives of Fugitive Slaves in Canada Related by Themselves* (Boston: John P. Jewett & Company, 1856), 30

9   Drew, *A North-side View of Slavery*, 60.

10   Michelle Alexander, *The New Jim Crow* (New York: New Press, 2010).

11   Laura Browder, *Her Best Shot: Women and Guns in America*. (Chapel Hill: University of North Carolina Press, 2006), 159.

12   Assata Shakur, *Assata: An Autobiography* (Chicago: Lawrence Hill, 2001), 260.

13   Shakur, *Assata*, 261.

M IS FOR MONSTER

1   Mary Shelley, "Introduction" (1831), *Frankenstein; or, The Modern Prometheus* (1818 text), ed. D. L. MacDonald and Kathleen Scherf (Peterborough, Canada: Broadview Press, 1999), 357.

2   Ellen Moers made the connection between Frankenstein and Mary Shelley's experience of pregnancy in her classic article "Female Gothic," in *The Endurance of Frankenstein: Essays on Mary Shelley's Novel*, ed. George Levine and U. C. Knoepflmacher (Oakland: University of California Press, 1979), 77–87.

3   Mary Shelley, *The Journals of Mary Shelley*, eds. Paula R. Feldman and Diana Scott-Kilvert (Oxford: Oxford University Press, 1987), 71.

4   Shelley, *Frankenstein*, 72.

N IS FOR NIGHTMARE

1   Torre Nielson, "Nightmares: A New Neurocognitive Model," *Sleep Medicine Reviews* 11 (2000): 295–310.

2   Primo Levi, *Survival in Auschwitz* (1947), trans. Stuart Woolf (New York: Touchstone, 1996).

3   Levi, *Survival in Auschwitz*, 60.

4   Levi, *Survival in Auschwitz*, 60.

5   Levi, *Survival in Auschwitz*, 60.

6   Philip Roth, "A Conversation with Primo Levi," in Levi, *Survival in Auschwitz*, 180.

7   Roth, "A Conversation with Primo Levi," 181.

8   Primo Levi and other distinguished Jewish personalities signed an open letter published in *La Stampa* that called for the withdrawal of Israeli troops from Lebanon and the recognition of "the right to self-determination of the Palestinian people." Levi also denounced the massacres in an interview with Giampaolo Pansa titled "Begin Should Go," published by *La Repubblica*, September 24, 1982, and republished in English in Primo Levi, *The Voice of Memory: Interviews 1961–1987*, eds. Marco Belpoliti and Robert Gordon, trans. Robert Gordon (New York: The New Press, 2001), 279–286.

9   In a 1984 interview with Gad Lerner published in *L'Espresso*, Levi again called for Israel to withdrawal from Lebanon and then went on to say: "Then it is just as urgent to stop further construction of settlements in the occupied territories. After that, as I was saying, I would cautiously but firmly move on a withdrawal from the West Bank and Gaza." Republished in Levi, *The Voice of Memory*, 291.

10   This scene is recounted in Pankaj Mishra's "The Shoah after Gaza," *London Review of Books* 46, no. 6 (March 21, 2024), https://www.lrb.co.uk/the-paper/v46/n06/pankaj-mishra/the-shoah-after-gaza.

O IS FOR OTOSCOPE

1   Interview with Dr. Ishani Rao, conducted February 2021. All quotations from Rao come from this interview, excerpts of which can be heard at Sharon Sliwinski, host, *Guardians of Sleep*, season 1, episode 1, "Dr. Rao," The Museum of Dreams, August 9, 2021, www.museumofdreams.org/guardians-of-sleep/2021/8/9/episode-one-dr-rao.

2   Ishani Rao and George Whittaker, *National Health Stories: Tales from the Front Line* (London: Independent Publishing Network, 2020).

3   Erik Homburger Erikson, "The Dream Specimen of Psychoanalysis," *Journal of the American Psychoanalytic Association* 2 (1954): 6.

4   Theodor Reik, *Listening with the Third Ear: The Inner Experience of an Analyst* (New York: Farrar, Straus, & Giroux, 1949).

5   Apart from the sources already noted, our method for listening to dreams was also influenced by Thomas Ogden's concept of reverie. See Thomas Ogden, *Reverie and Interpretation: Sensing Something Human* (London: Routledge, 1997).

6   Erikson, "The Dream Specimen of Psychoanalysis," 5–56.

7   Freud does not explicitly state that the patient in his dream, whom he calls "Irma," was his patient Emma Eckstein, but most scholars understand the dream this way, especially after Freud's doctor published his account. See Max Schur, "Some Additional 'Day Residues' of 'the Specimen Dream of Psychoanalysis,'" in *Psychoanalysis: General Psychology. Essays in Honor of Heinz Hartmann*, ed. R. M. Loewenstein, L. M. Newman, M. Schur, A. J. Solnit (New York: International Universities Press, 1966), 45–85.

8   Lawrence Blum, "Physicians' Goodness and Guilt: Emotional Challenges of Practicing Medicine," *JAMA Internal Medicine* 179, no. 5 (2019): 607–608.

P IS FOR PRINCESS DIANA

1   Interview with Kavita conducted February 2021. All quotations from come from this interview, excerpts of which can be heard at Sharon Sliwinski, host, *Guardians of Sleep*, season 1, episode 2, "Kavita," The Museum of Dreams, August 10, 2021, https://www.museumofdreams.org/guardians-of-sleep/2021/8/9/episode-2-kavita.

2   Judith Butler, "Precariousness and Grievability," *Verso* (blog), November 16, 2015, https://www.versobooks.com/en-ca/blogs/news/2339-judith-butler-precariousness-and-grievability.

Q IS FOR QUACKERY

1   Book 4 of Hippocrates's treatise *De Victu* (*On Regimen*) deals with the use of dreams for medical prognosis. For discussions of this work, see P. J. van der Eijk, "Divination, Prognosis and Prophylaxis: The Hippocratic Work 'On Dreams' (*De Victu* 4) and Its Near Eastern Background," in *Magic and Rationality in Near Eastern and Graeco-Roman Medicine*, ed. H. F. J. Horstmanshoff and M. Stol (Leiden: Brill, 2004).

2   Christian Brockmann, "A God and Two Humans on Matters of Medicine: Asclepius, Galen, and Aelius Aristides," in *In Praise of Asclepius: Aelius Aristides, Selected Prose Hymns*, ed. Donald A. Russell, Michael Trapp, and Heinz-Günther Nesselrath (Tübingen, Germany: Mohr Siebeck, 2016), 115–128. See also Frances Flannery's work, especially "Talitha Qum! An Exploration of the Image of Jesus as Healer-Physician-Savior in the Synoptic Gospels in Relation to the Asclepius Cult," in *Coming Back to Life: The Permeability of Past and Present, Mortality and Immortality, Death and Life in the Ancient Mediterranean*, ed. Frederick Tappenden and Carly Daniel-Hughes (Montreal: McGill University Library and Archives, 2017), 407–434.

3   Deirdre Barrett, *The Committee of Sleep: How Artists, Scientists, and Athletes Use Their Dreams for Creative Problem-Solving—and How You Can Too* (New York: Crown/Random House, 2001), 123.

4   Sigmund Freud, "A Metapsychological Supplement to the Theory of Dreams," in *The Standard Edition of the Complete Psychological Works of Sigmund Freud,* vol. 14, ed. James Strachey (London: Hogarth, 1955), 223.

5   For a discussion of the history of the concept of disease, see Eric J. Cassell, *The Nature of Suffering and the Goals of Medicine* (Oxford: Oxford University Press, 2004).

6   George L. Engel, "The Need for a New Medical Model: A Challenge for Biomedicine," *Science* 196, no. 4286 (April 8, 1977): 129–136, reprinted in *Psychodynamic Psychiatry* 40, no. 3 (September 2012): 387.

7   Gabor Maté, *The Myth of Normal: Trauma, Illness, and Healing in a Toxic Culture* (Toronto: Knopf, 2022).

8   Charles Stewart, *Dreaming and Historical Consciousness in Island Greece* (Chicago: University of Chicago Press).

9   Edward W. Said, *The World, the Text, and the Critic* (Cambridge, MA: Harvard University Press, 1983).

R IS FOR REFUGE

1   Magnus Wennman's 2016 series, "Where the Children Sleep," first appeared in the Swedish newsmagazine *Aftonbladet*, https://darbarnensover.aftonbladet.se/chapter/english-version and subsequently circulated through a partnership with the UNHCR, the United Nations Refugee Agency, June 1, 2016, https://www.unhcr.org/us/news/stories/where-children-sleep.

2   Arielle Moncure, "Behind the Scenes of 'Where the Children Sleep,'" UNHCR, the United Nations Refugee Agency, June 30, 2016, https://www.unhcr.org/hk/en/3274-behind-the-scenes-of-where-the-children-sleep.html.

3   Magnus Wennman (@magnuswennman), "Where Is Lamar?,"
Instagram, January 10, 2019, https://www.instagram.com/p/Bscsy
_RlOBN/?hl=en.

4   Christina Sharpe, *Ordinary Notes* (Toronto: Alfred A. Knopf, 2023), 36.

5   Martha Rosler, "In, around, and Afterthoughts (on Documentary
Photography)" (1981), in *The Contest of Meaning: Critical Histories of
Photography*, ed. Richard Bolton (Cambridge, MA: MIT Press, 1990).

6   John Berger, "Photographs of Agony" (1972), in *About Looking*
(New York: Vintage, 1991), 44.

7   UNHCR [United Nations Refugee Agency], "Figures at a Glance,"
June 13, 2024, https://www.unhcr.org/about-unhcr/who-we-are/figures
-glance.

8   Hannah Arendt, *The Origins of Totalitarianism* (1951) (New York:
Schocken, 2004), 376.

9   Magnus Wennman's film *Fatima's Drawings* (2016) is available on
Vimeo at https://vimeo.com/159034152.

10   Debarati Guha-Sapir et al., "Patterns of Civilian and Child Deaths
Due to War-Related Violence in Syria: A Comparative Analysis from the
Violation Documentation Center Dataset, 2011–16," *The Lancet* 5, no. 1
(January 2018): e103–e110, https://www.thelancet.com/action showPdf?pii
=S2214-109X%2817%2930469-2.

11   Jean-François Lyotard, *The Differend: Phrases in Dispute* (1983),
trans. Georges Van Den Abbeele (Minneapolis: University of Minnesota
Press, 1988), 5.

12   Stefan Zweig, *The World of Yesterday* (1942), trans. Anthea Bell
(London: Pushkin Press, 2009), 417.

13   My phrasing is indebted here to Georges Didi-Huberman's
discussion of a different dream archive in *Survival of the Fireflies*, trans.
Lia Swope Mitchell (Minneapolis: University of Minnesota Press, 2018),
74.

S IS FOR SUICIDE

1   Billy-Ray Belcourt, *This Wound Is a World* (Minneapolis: University
of Minnesota Press, 2019).

2   Billy-Ray Belcourt, *A History of My Brief Body* (Columbus, OH: Two
Dollar Radio, 2020), 104.

3   Belcourt, *A History of My Brief Body*, 102 and 104 respectively.

4   I borrow here from Sakue Shimohira's testimony, which appears
in the documentary film *White Light/Black Rain: The Destruction of
Hiroshima and Nagasaki* , directed and produced by Steven Okazaki
(HBO, 2007). Shimohira describes how, as a ten-year-old, she and her

sister survived the US bombing of Nagasaki, the only members of their family to survive. A few months after the bombing, Shimohira's sister took her life by jumping in front of a train. Although she says that her life has not contained a single moment of joy since the time of the bombing, she chose to live: "There are two kinds of courage—the courage to die and the courage to live. My sister had the courage to die. I chose the courage to live."

5   Belcourt, *A History of My Brief Body*, 105.

6   Christian Sharpe, *Ordinary Notes* (Toronto: Alfred A. Knopf, 2023), 312.

7   Euripides, *Medea*, ed. and trans. Diane J. Rayor (Cambridge: Cambridge University Press, 2013), 53.

8   Belcourt, *A History of My Brief Body*, 106.

9   Sigmund Freud, "An Outline of Psychoanalysis" (1940 [1938]), in *The Standard Edition of the Complete Psychological Works of Sigmund Freud*, vol. 23, ed. James Strachey (London: Hogarth Press, 1964), 204.

10   Sigmund Freud, "Splitting of the Ego in the Process of Defense," *Standard Edition*, vol. 23, 277.

T IS FOR TRANS

1   Paul B. Preciado, "Introduction," *An Apartment on Uranus: Chronicles of the Crossing*, trans. Charlotte Mandell (South Pasadena, CA: Semiotext(e), 2020), 34.

2   Preciado, "Introduction," *An Apartment on Uranus*, 33.

3   Paul B. Preciado, "A Letter from a Trans Man to the Old Sexual Regime," trans. Simon Pleasance, *Texte Zur Kunst*, January 22, 2018, https://www.textezurkunst.de/en/articles/letter-trans-man-old-sexual-regime-paul-b-preciado.

4   Paul B. Preciado, "One Day We'll See Assigning Gender at Birth as Brutal," interview by Marie Katherine Tramontana, *I-D*, March 12, 2020, https://i-d.co/article/paul-b-preciado-one-day-well-see-assigning-gender-at-birth-as-brutal.

5   Preciado, "Introduction," *An Apartment on Uranus*, 36.

6   Preciado, "Introduction," *An Apartment on Uranus*, 34.

7   My data comes from Trans Legislation Tracker, which complies data on US legislation. The organization has helped news organizations (including the *New York Times* and *Teen Vogue*), university scholars, independent researchers, and US government officials to bring awareness to the historic rise in antitrans legislation. Trans Legislation Tracker, https://translegislation.com/about, accessed February 1, 2024.

8   Preciado, "Introduction," *An Apartment on Uranus*, 21.

U IS FOR UTOPIA

1   Walidah Imarisha, "Introduction," in *Octavia's Brood: Science Fiction Stories from Social Justice Movements*, ed. Walidah Imarisha and adrienne maree brown (Oakland, CA: AK Press, 2015). brown is one of the most powerful and extensive commentators on Butler's work. See Toshi Reagon and adrienne maree brown, *Octavia's Parables*, podcast, https://www.readingoctavia.com.

2   Octavia E. Butler, "The Book of Martha," (2003) in *Bloodchild and Other Stories*, 2nd ed. (New York: Seven Stories Press, 2005).

3   Butler, "The Book of Martha," 191.

4   Butler, "The Book of Martha," 192.

5   Butler, "The Book of Martha," 197.

6   Butler, "The Book of Martha," 210 and 211 respectively.

7   Butler, Afterword to "The Book of Martha," 214.

8   For a good overview of the scholarly debates about utopia, see Ruth Levitas, *The Concept of Utopia* (Witney, UK: Peter Lang Ltd., 2011).

V IS FOR VEGETABLES

1   Sigmund Freud, *The Interpretation of Dreams* (1900), in *The Standard Edition of the Complete Psychological Works of Sigmund Freud*, vol. 4, ed. James Strachey (London: Hogarth Press, 1953), 183.

2   Although Freud does not record any associations to the "black color" of the asparagus, it is worth pointing out that scholars have noted the unacknowledged and yet foundational role of race in the psychoanalytic canon. The literature is extensive, but specifically in relation to dreams, see Christopher Lane, ed., *The Psychoanalysis of Race* (New York: Columbia, 1998); Jean Walton, *Fair Sex, Savage Dreams: Race, Psychoanalysis, Sexual Difference* (Durham: Duke University Press, 2001); Celia Brickman, *Race in Psychoanalysis: Aboriginal Populations in the Mind* (London: Routledge, 2017); Sheldon George and Derek Hook, eds. *Lacan and Race: Racism, Identity, and Psychoanalytic Theory* (London: Routledge, 2021).

3   Freud, *The Interpretation of Dreams*, 185, n. 1.

W IS FOR WHITE WOLVES

1   Sergei Pankejeff is the English transliteration of the Russian name Сергей Панкéев.

2   Sigmund Freud, "From the History of an Infantile Neurosis," in *The Standard Edition of the Complete Psychological Works of Sigmund Freud*, vol. 17, ed. James Strachey (London: Hogarth Press, 1955), 3–122.

3   Sigmund Freud, "From the History of an Infantile Neurosis," 29.

4   Sergei Pankejeff, "Memoirs of the Wolf-Man," in *The Wolf-man and Sigmund Freud*, ed. and trans. Muriel Gardiner (London: Karnac, 1989), 5.

5   Pankejeff, "Memoirs of the Wolf-Man," 5

6   Pankejeff, "Memoirs of the Wolf-Man," 25.

7   Freud, "From the History of an Infantile Neurosis," 20.

8   See Nicholas Abraham and Maria Torok, *The Wolf-Man's Magic Word: A Cryptonymy* (1976), trans. Nicholas Rand (Minneapolis: University of Minnesota, 1986); George Dimock, "Anna and the Wolf-Man: Rewriting Freud's Case History," *Representations* no. 50 (Spring 1995): 53–75.

9   Freud, "From the History of an Infantile Neurosis," 42, n. 2.

10   Gabor Maté, *The Myth of Normal: Trauma, Illness and Healing in a Toxic Culture* (Toronto: Knopf, 2022).

11   Sigmund Freud, "Further Remarks on the Neuro-psychoses of Defense" (1896), in *The Standard Edition of the Complete Psychological Works of Sigmund Freud*, vol. 3, ed. James Strachey (London: Hogarth Press, 1962), 164.

12   Didier Anzieu, *The Skin Ego: A Psychoanalytic Approach to Self* (1985), trans. Chris Turner (New Haven, CT: Yale University Press, 1989).

X IS FOR XANAX

1   Asa Engström et al., "The Meaning of Critical Illness for People Suffering from COVID-19: When a Frightening Unreality Becomes Reality," *Qualitative Health Research* 32, no. 1 (2022): 135–144; Serena Scarpelli et al., "Nightmares in People with COVID-19: Did Coronavirus Infect Our Dreams?," *Nature and Science of Sleep* 14 (2022): 93–108.

2   Interview with Shelley conducted February 2021. All quotations from come from this interview, excerpts of which can be heard at Sharon Sliwinski, host, *Guardians of Sleep*, season 1, episode 6, "The Guardians," The Museum of Dreams, August 12, 2022, https://www.museumofdreams .org/guardians-of-sleep/2022/8/12/episode-6-the-guardians.

3   My phrasing here is indebted to Kelly Boivin's beautiful book, *We Dream Medicine Dreams* (Toronto: Scholastic, 2021), but the idea that dreams are medicine is widely held among Indigenous cultures from Turtle Island and beyond.

4   L. Perogamvros et al., "Sleep and Dreaming Are for Important Matters," *Frontiers in Psychology* 4 (July 2013): 474, https://doi.org/10.3389 /fpsyg.2013.00474.

5   Ivan Illich, *Limits to Medicine. Medical Nemesis: The Expropriation of Health* (New York: Penguin Books, 1977).

6   Eduardo Duran, *Healing the Soul Wound: Trauma-Informed Counseling for Indigenous Communities*, 2nd ed. (New York: News College Press, 2019), 16. Other medical practitioners who have researched the healing power of dreams include the palliative care doctor, Christopher Kerr. See his book with Carine Mardorossian, *Death Is But a Dream: Finding Hope and Meaning at Life's End* (Toronto: Penguin, 2020).

Y IS FOR YOU

1   Artemidorus, *The Interpretation of Dreams,* trans. Martin Hammond (Oxford: Oxford University Press, 2020), 4.

2   Tricia Hersey, *Rest Is Resistance: A Manifesto* (New York: Little Brown Spark, 2022).

3   Ludwig Binswanger, "Dream and Existence" (1930) in Michael Foucault and Ludwig Binswanger, *Dream and Existence,* ed. Keith Hoeller, trans. Forrest Williams (New Jersey: Humanities Press, 1993), 102.

4   Sigmund Freud, *New Introductory Lectures* (1933 [1932]), in *The Standard Edition of the Complete Psychological Works of Sigmund Freud*, vol. 22 (London: Hogarth Press, 1964), 21.

5   Ella Freeman Sharpe, *Dream Analysis* (London: Hogarth Press, 1959), 18.

6   Clarence B. Jones, *Behind the Dream: The Making of the Speech That Transformed a Nation* (New York: Saint Martin's Griffin, 2012).

7   Ella Baker Center for Human Rights, "Who Was Ella Baker?" https://ellabakercenter.org/who-was-ella-baker.

8   J. Todd Moyne, *Ella Baker: Community Organizer of the Civil Rights Movement* (Lanham: Rowman & Littlefield, 2013), 3.

Z IS FOR ZED

1   Marcus Aurelius, *Meditations,* trans. Gregory Hays (New York: Random House, 2002), 76.

2   Marcus Aurelius, *Meditations,* 71.